AF543148

RESTRUCTURING OF STATE LEVEL PUBLIC ENTERPRISES

RESTRUCTURING OF STATE LEVEL PUBLIC ENTERPRISES

A Study

By
R.K. Mishra
B. Navin

ANMOL PUBLICATIONS PVT. LTD.
NEW DELHI - 110 002 (INDIA)

ANMOL PUBLICATIONS PVT. LTD.
4374/4B, Ansari Road, Daryaganj
New Delhi - 110 002
Ph.: 3261597, 3278000
www.anmolbooks.com

Restructuring of State Level Public Enterprises
© Authors

First Edition, 2002

ISBN 81-261-1127-5

[All rights reserved. No part of this publication may be reproduced, stored in a retrieval system or transmitted, in any form or by any means, mechanical, photocopying, recording or otherwise, without prior written permission of the publisher.]

PRINTED IN INDIA

Published by J.L. Kumar for Anmol Publications Pvt. Ltd., New Delhi - 110 002 and Printed at Mehra Offset Press, Delhi.

Contents

Preface

The State Level Public Enterprises (SLPEs) are an important component of the economy of Madhya Pradesh (MP). The restructuring of SLPEs is an integral part of the economic reforms initiated by the State Government. This study presents the State of select SLPEs in MP, their institutional structure, goernance relations and scope and time table for future reforms. As a prelude, the study provides a backdrop of the economy of MP. The information contained in this study has been obtained from both the primary and secondary sources for the period 1992-93 to 1996-97. Discussions were held with top level State functionaries dealing with SLPEs and the Secretary, Department of Public Enterprise, Government of MP. A direct rapport was established with the Chief Executive Officers of SLPEs and subsequently a number of meetings were held individually with them. An exhaustive data sheet was designed to collect unpublished data and information from SLPEs. A detailed questionnaire was to formulated to elicit information regarding the various terms of reference of the study. The Annual Reports and Accounts, Articles of Association and Memoranda of Association were collected from the SLPEs for the said period subject to furnishing of these documents. The reports published by the Accountant General, MP, Government of MP and the Committee on Public Undertakings of the State Legislative Assembly of MP as also the news items that appeared were referred to. The analysis and conclusions of the study have faced some critical limitations. The information furnished in the data sheets was unconfirmed accounts in most of the cases. The information so furnished was also found at variance with the information contained in published annual reports and accounts in some cases. In some cases, despite repeated requests, information regarding the various aspects of the study was not furnished. Due to lack of preparedness, several enterprises delayed the furnishing of information.

1

Madhya Pradesh State Road Transport Corporation

Introduction

Madhya Pradesh (MP) is the largest State in India with an area of 4.44 lakh square metre divided into 45 districts with a population of 72.7 million. Over 45% of its land area is cultivable, of which 13% is under irrigation. The economy of MP is agriculture based. Jowar, wheat, rice and grain are the main food crops. Oilseeds, cotton, soybean and sugarcane are the main commercial crops. The State is endowed with ample natural resources and has good potential for accelerated industrial development. Coal, iron ore, limestone, dolomite, bauxite, copper, phosphorite, feldspar, asbestos, diamond and manganese ore are the principal mineral deposits. The State Government has announced its new industrial policy and action plan in May 1994.

RTC Act

The public transport sector provides essential services required for the development of the economy, industry and agriculture. Transport is a State subject under the Constitution of India. The Government of India enacted the Road Transport Corporations Act in the year 1950 to provide, secure and promote the provision of an efficient, adequate, economical and properly coordinated system of road transport services in the State which shall act on business principles in carrying on its undertaking.

MPSRTC

The Government of MP formed a passenger transport organisation in 1962 in the public sector under Section 3 of the Road Transport Corporation's (RTC's Act), 1950 called the Madhya Pradesh State Road Transport Corporation (MPSRTC). It is a successor corporation to the erstwhile Madhya Bharat Roadways (MBR) and Central Provinces Transport Services (CPTS). At the time of formation, the capital contribution from the State and Central Governments was in the ratio of 3:1 respectively. This ratio was later revised to 2:1 during April 1969. The Corporation has to work within the framework of several statutory enactments, such as the Motor Vehicles Act, Motor Transport Workers' Act, Factories Act, Shops and Establishments Act, etc. The working of MPSRTC is governed by the MPSRTC Rules, 1962, framed under the RTC's Act.

Road Transport Sector

Transport is fast emerging as an important segment of the economy and is a growing service industry in a highly competitive arena. While long-distance passenger transport is provided by airways and railways, other passenger transport has to be provided by road transport services. Such services must be efficient, competitive and meet customer needs. There is, therefore, ample scope and need for MPSRTC to manage passenger transport effectively to take advantage of opportunities of growth. MPSRTC has over a quarter of a century's experience and has developed considerable infrastructure. The fare structure of the Corporation is quite favourable compared to fare structure obtaining in similar Road Transport Corporations in other States. The inability of MPSRTC to generate surplus revenues by reducing costs, rationalising operations, improving efficiency and replacement of buses in time has stood in the way of continued and self-sustained growth. However, there is scope for mobilising resources not only for maintaining its present operations but for further rapid expansion. In the process, it can reduce the burden on the State exchequer and become a self-sustained Corporation.

Data Used for Analysis

The analysis of MPSRTC is based on published data and information provided by the Corporation to the Consultants. The data for the years 1992-93 to 1995-96 are based on audited Annual Accounts of MPSRTC, while that of 1996-97 are unaudited and provisional figures.

Organisational Structure

MPSRTC has a three tier-organisational structure, i.e. Corporate Office, Divisions and Depots. In the Corporate Office, the Managing Director who is the Chief Executive is assisted by 11 Heads of Department. The Corporation has 11 Divisions, comprising of 2 Central Workshops, 3 Regional Workshops, 6 Divisional Workshops, and a Central Stores and Purchase Division. Every Division is headed by a Divisional Manager (DVM). The DVM is assisted by 7 Functional Junior Managers. It has 56 Operating Depots, 13 Sub-depots and a Printing Press. At the Depot-level, the Depot Manager (DM) is assisted by 6 persons who are in charge of different functions.

Fleet and Operations

MPSRTC holds 71 Approved Schemes under the Motor Vehicles Act to serve passengers in different parts of the State. A fleet of 1912 buses at the minimum level of operations, and 2945 buses at maximum level of operations, is required to service the Approved Schemes. Though the Corporation has a total fleet of 2434 buses, inclusive of 80 hired buses, it is, however, operating only 1686 buses. As a result, the Corporation is unable to run 29% of Approved Routes under the MV Act. MPSRTC has 21,743 employees and is scheduled to operate 7.62 km per day, but operates only 4.75 lakh km per day, or 63% of the scheduled operations.

Route Pattern

MP has a total route length of 94886 km, while MPSRTC which operates in the National area, covers 7000 km. *The nationalised route accounts for 4.5% of total route distance* while the Railways cater to only 1.5%. Thus, only 6% of the route length is exclusively covered by the public sector.

The road route pattern on various categories of roads in the State is as follows:

Table 1.1

Type of Route	*No. of Routes*	*%*
National Highways	137	10
State Highways	503	38
District Highways	128	10
National and State Highways combined	270	20
National and District Highways combined	92	7
State and District Highways combined	141	11
National, State and District Highways combined	47	4
Total	1318	100

Source: MPSRTC's reply to Consultant's Questionnaire

Route Utilisation

MP State has 6756 routes, of which 1318 (19.5%) have been allocated to MPSRTC which is operating only 712 routes, i.e. 54%. Of the remaining 600 routes, MPSRTC is marginally operating in 224 routes, while 382 routes or 29% of allocated routes are not operated at all.

Passenger Amenities

MPSRTC has built 434 Bus Stands and 189 Bus Shelters (Pick-up Stands) as Passenger Amenities. Viewed against the extent of the State of MP and routes that MPSRTC is operating, these Passenger Amenities are not adequate. The Corporation should, however, plan to consolidate its operations by pressing new buses into service, running on all routes and strengthening preventive maintenance practices before undertaking any extensive investments on passenger amenities.

Share of Transport Operations

The share of MPSRTC in the passenger transport operations in the State is as follows, whole is as follows:

Table 1.2

Share of Private Sector and MPSRTC in Passenger Transport

Type of Operation	*Total No. of Buses in MP State*	*No. of Buses in Private Sector*	*% of Total*	*No. of MPSRTC Buses*	*% to Total*
Stage Carriages	9796	7350	75	2446	25
Contact Carriages (Deluxe Operations)	573	567	99	6	1
Mini Buses	18993	18993	100	Nil	00
Motor Cabs, Taxis & Mini Cabs	8206	8206	100	Nil	00
Total	37568	35116	93	2452	07

Source: MPSRTC's reply to Consultant's Questionnaire

MPSRTC has a good market share of 25% in respect of Stage Carriages, 1% in Contract Carriage, and none in Mini Buses, Motor Cabs, Taxis and Mini Cabs. In all, the Corporation accounts for only 7% of transport operations in the State.

Fleet Strength and Off-Road Vehicles

The fleet strength, the percentage of buses operated and off-road is a good index of the operational efficiency of a transport corporation. The Statement of Fleet Strength Vs. Vehicles Off-Road for five years is given in Table 1.3.

Table 1.3
Fleet Strength and Off-Road Vehicles

Year	*Fleet Strength*	*Average Age in Years*	*No. of Buses Off-Road*	*% of Off-Road Buses*	*No. of Buses on Road*	*New Buses Added**
1992-93	2859	8.01	613	21	2246	NA
1993-94	2775	8.17	543	18	2232	116
1994-95	2667	8.60	493	18	2174	91
1995-96	2584	9.30	643	23	1941	50
1996-97	2434	9.79	818	34	1686	72

*Against Replacements
Source: MPSRTC's reply to Consultant's Questionnaire

The fleet strength has declined from 2859 in 1992-93 to 2434 in 1996-97, i.e. by 15%. The number of business on road in 1992-93 was 2246 while in 1996-97 it was only 1686, i.e. a reduction of 28%. *The figure of on-road buses at 66% may be compared with the All-India average of vehicles held to vehicles on road which is around 90%.*

The off-road vehicles increased from 613 in 1992-93 to 818 in 1996-97, i.e. by 33%. Buses off-road to fleet strength has increased from 21% in 1992-93 to 34% in 1996-97. *One-third of the fleet of MPSRTC i.e. 818 buses are off-road,* indicating that two-thirds of the buses on road are being flogged without adequate arrangements for preventive maintenance or replacement.

The average age of fleet which was 8.01 years in 1992-93 has risen to 9.79 years in 1996-97, leading to heavy maintenance expenditure on over-aged vehicles besides running the risk of frequent break downs, cancellations of services and inconvenience to passengers. As the age of vehicles increases, there has to be a proper policy of replacement of buses. There is also precipitious fall in replacement of buses from 1992-93 to 1995-96 calling for an immediate Bus Replacement Policy in the Corporation. However, some attempts have been made during 1996-97 to reverse this trend.

Fleet Utilisation

The kilometres operated per day, route schedules and off-road vehicles, as well as the composition and age of fleet, gives the efficacy of fleet utilisation. Fleet utilisation is also a function of health of buses, breakdowns, speedy availability of vital spares and preventive maintenance practices. MPSRTC has a fleet of 2434 buses as on March 31, 1997, which came down to 2294 in December 1997. Of these, 6 are Deluxe Buses, 832 are operated either as express buses in night operation or on inter-state long-distance routes. The remaining (1456) are operated as ordinary buses. Of them, 1206 buses are of average age of 9 years. 794 buses are off-road requiring heavy repairs. Fleet utilisation has gradually come down from 82% in 1994-95 to 75% in 1995-96 and 69% in 1996-97. *This downward trend in fleet utilisation is primarily ascribable to non-replacement of buses, over-aged buses, off-road buses and inadequate preventive maintenance practices.*

WORKSHOP AND TYRE SHOP PERFORMANCE

Workshop Performance

Workshop performance is usually assessed by ascertaining the number of buses fabricated or units (buses, engines, gear boxes) overhauled, expenditure incurred on spare and materials, expenditure on labour, and cost per unit overhauled. It is the workshop's efficiency which literally keeps vehicles moving. It is a standard practice to review the operability of buses and grade them for replacement. Vehicle Scrapping and Vehicle Replacement Policy has to be dovetailed with preventive maintenance practices to ensure robust health of fleet. The following table gives the picture on these parameters in MPSRTC.

Table 1.4
Workshop Performance

S. No.	Parameter	Unit	1994-95	1995-96	1996-97	% Increase/ Decline
1.	Buses overhauled	No.	890	843	631	(-) 29
2.	Engine overhauled	No.	2471	2041	1619	(0) 34
3.	Gear boxes overhauled	No.	4923	2453	3550	(-) 28
4.	Equivalence units (engines)	No.	985	491	710	(-) 28
5.	Total engines (2+4)	No.	3456	2532	2329	(-) 33
6.	Equivalence units (buses)	No.	532	390	358	(-) 30
7.	Total C/o buses (1+6)	No.	1422	1233	989	(-) 30
8.	Expenditure on spares/ materials	Rs./ Lakhs	818	819	799	(-) 2
9.	Expenditure on labour	"	1234	1339	1519	23
10.	Total Workshop expenditure	"	2052	2158	2318	13
11.	Average cost per bus	"	144534	175415	234121	62
12.	% Increase over previous year	%	-	21	33	-

Note: Equivalence Factor:

5	gear boxes	=	1 engine
6.5	engines	=	1 bus
32.5	gear box	=	1 bus

Source: MPSRTC's reply to Consultant's Questionnaire

Workshop performance had deteriorated in respect of buses fabricated or overhauled. Engine overhaul came down by 34% and gear box overhauling by 28%. Cost of overhauling a bus had increased in 1995-96 by 21% and by 33% in 1996-97 when compared to the previous years. Expenditure on labour increased by 23% though there was 30% decrease in activity.

Equivalence Factors

As standards have not been prescribed or are not available in MPSRTC, Equivalence Unit have been worked out based on APSRTC's standards for the limited purpose of arriving at cost of overhauling of a bus.

Table 1.5
Cost of Overhauling Bus

Parameter	*Unit*	*Complete Overhaul*		
		Gear Box	*Engine*	*Bus*
Average labour hours required	Hrs	40	300	2200
Rate per labour hour	Rs.	50	50	50
Labour charges	Rs.	2000	15000	110000
Average materials consumption	Rs.	6000	21000	110000
Overhead charges (100% of labour charges)	Rs.	2000	15000	110000
Total cost of overhaul	Rs.	10000	51000	330000

Note: Equivalence Factor: 5 gear boxes = 1 engine
6.5 engines = 1 bus
32.5 gear boxes = 1 bus

During 1997-98 in APSRTC, the cost of overhauling has been as follows:

Gear box : Rs. 7,750
Engine : Rs. 33,850
Bus : Rs. 2,75,650

Tyre Shop Performance

Tyre maintenance practices have to be accorded importance as MPSRTC spends Rs. 1100 lakhs per annum on tyres. Proper tyre maintenance practices extend the average maiden life of tyre and improves its retreadability factor. Tyres Shop Performance for three years ending March 31, 1997 is as follows:

Table 1.6
Tyre Shop Performance

Parameter	*Unit*	*1994-95*	*1995-96*	*1996-97*
Price of one new tyre, tube, flap	Rs.	6500	6800	7150
Average km obtained from new tyre in maiden life	Km	45483	45171	44357
Cost per km (CPK) of new tyre	Paise	14	15	16
Tyres retreaded/recapped	No.	25049	22643	19232
Expenditure on raw materials	Rs./Lakhs	208	237	222
Expenditure on labour	"	12	15	15
Expenditure on overheads	"	12	15	15
Total expenditure	"	2421	277	253
Average cost per RT/RC	Rs.	965	1180	1314
Average km obtained from RT/RC tyres (cold process)	km	28117	28241	27725
Average km obtained from RT/RC tyres (hot process)	km	15316	18273	18807
Total km obtained from RT/RC tyres	km	43433	46514	46532
Average km obtained (cold/hot)	km	21716	23257	23266

Legend: RT = Retreading; RC = Recapping
Source: MPSRTC's reply to Consultant's Questionnaire

Tyre maintenance should be totally reviewed and a Good Practice Manual drawup afresh to ensure maximum tyre life through better Retreadability? Factor (i.e. more number of times retreading/recapping each tyre) besides obtaining maximum kilometres in the maiden life of tyres.

Key Result Areas -- Comparative Position

The overall efficiency of MPSRTC has been evaluated on ten Key Result Areas shown in Table 1.7. Figures of MPSRTC have been compared with figures of Maharashtra State Road Transport Corporation (MSRTC) and Andhra Pradesh State Road Transport Corporation (APSRTC). All Key Result Areas are compared on the basis of per kilometre of operation.

Table 1.7
Key Result Areas

S. No.	*Key Results Area*	*MPSRTC*	*APSRTC*	*MSRTC*	*Likely order of savings in MPSRTC if compared with best performance Rs./Lakhs*
1.	Gross Earnings	9.68	9.51	9.80	
2.	Gross Expenditure				
	- Personnel				
	- Fuel				
	- Tyres				
	- Workshop				
	- Stores				
	- Lubricants				
	- Taxes				
	- Interest				
	- Miscellaneous				
	- Depreciation				
	Total Gross Expenditure				
3.	Surplus/Deficit (1-2)				

Note: Lubricants are included in Fuel in MSRTC. Workshop expenditure on MPSRTC is not available.

Source: Published Statistics of 3 Corporations

It may be noted that APSRTC's performance is comparatively the best in 8 out of 10 criteria. It is, however, incurring slightly higher expenditure on tyres. More expenditure on depreciation is due to additional provision of 20% made to meet price escalation in the year of replacement of bus over and above the normal chargeable depreciation.

Further, the average age of fleet in APSRTC is about 4.5 years while in MPSRTC it is over 9.0 years.

MPSRTC is incurring more expenditure on Personnel, Workshop Maintenance, Stores, Lubricants, Taxes and Interest on Loans. MSRTC, like APSRTC, is making extra provision to meet price escalation in the year of replacement of buses. It may be noted that MSRTC is incurring more expenditure on Personnel and Stores when compared to MPSRTC. In respect of Fuel, Tyres, Taxes, Interest and Miscellaneous Expenses, MSRTC is performing better than MPSRTC.

There is large scope for improvement in key result areas by MPSRTC. If MPSRTC achieves the level of performance already achieved by APSRTC, it can save Rs. 5248 lakhs per year in expenditure. With some revisions of fare, MPSRTC has good scope to turn around with appropriate restructuring and professional management.

Capital Structure

Under Section 23(1) of the RTC's Act, 1950, the Central and State Governments may provide to a Corporation established by the State Government any capital that may be required by the Corporation in such proportion as may be agreed to by both Governments. The capital contribution agreed to be subscribed between the State and Central Governments at the time of formation of MPSRTC in 1962 was in the ratio of 3:1 respectively. This ratio was subsequently revised to 2:1 during April 1969. The Corporation has to pay interest at the rate of 6.25% p.a. on capital contribution to the State and Central Governments irrespective of the fact whether the Corporation made a profit or loss. In effect, this capital contribution is in the nature of *preference capital.*

The issue of conversion of capital contribution into Equity was under consideration with the Government of India who agreed to the representations made by the SRTCs and decided on for conversion of Capital into Equity with effect from April 1, 1996. This conversion was subject to payment of dividend on the equity at a maximum rate of 3% in the year(s) in which the Corporation makes a profit. As MPSRTC is in default of payment of interest for the last seven years, capital contribution and share capital are shown separately in their Balance Sheet. The present Equity Capital of MPSRTC, including share capital contribution from the State and Central Governments is shown in Table 1.8.

Table 1.8
Equity Capital of MPSRTC

Share of	*Capital Contribution*	*Share Capital*	*Total*	*%*
State Government				
Central Government				
Total				

Source: MPSRTC's Annual Accounts for 1996-97

It will be noticed that shareholding between the State and Centre is 4:1 respectively. MPSRTC has not been paying interest on outstanding capital contribution or divided on equity for the last seven years.

Debt of MPSRTC

The debt as on March 31, 1997 was as follows:

Table 1.9
Debt of MPSRTC

S.No.	*Term Loan from*	*Rs./Lakhs*	*%*
A.	Banks		
B.	Others-LIC		
C.	Total		

Source: MPSRTC's reply to Consultant's Questionnaire

MPSRTC owes Rs. 2066 lakhs, of which 61% is due to banks/financial institutions and 39% to LIC.

Debt-Equity Ratio

If the total Share Capital and Capital Contribution is taken as Equity, the Debt-Equity Ratio works out to be 0.11:1, i.e. 2066:18236.

MPSRTC has a favourable debt-equity ratio and could draw term loans for much-needed augmention of fleet to improve revenues and reduce costs by better deployment of surplus manpower, but for its unhealthy Balance Sheet.

Undischarged Liabilities

MPSRTC has been in default of payments aggregating Rs. 35210 lakhs for the last seven years to Government, banks and others as given below:

Table 1.10
Undischarged Liabilities

S. No.	*Details of Liabilities*	*Rs./Lakhs*	*%*

Source: MPSRTC's reply to Consultant's Questionnaire

Due to the large unsettled or undischarged liabilities, MPSRTC has not been able to raise substantial term loans from banks or financial institutions. The liability of Rs. 35210 lakhs against an annual turnover of Rs.17379 lakhs is a matter of concern. It may be recalled that MPSRTC is able to operate only two-thirds of its fleet. 794 buses, or a third of the fleet is off-road and unable to generate much-needed revenues. They can be repaired to the extent found economical and put to use to increase revenues. The situation warrants settlement of liabilities and restructuring of capital in consultation with financial institutions and the Central and State Governments.

FINANCIAL PERFORMANCE

Financial Position

The Financial Position covering the period of five years from 1992-93 to 1996-97 is given at Annexure-I.

LIABILITIES

Funds:

MPSRTC is maintaining five funds, viz., Third Party Liability Fund, Staff Welfare Fund, Contribution to Employees Provident Fund, Employment Deposit Fund, and Depreciation Fund. It will be seen from Annexure-I that in 1993-94 and 1994-95 the funds provision has increased by 12% and 11% respectively compared to 1992-93. But in 1995-96 there is a drop of 27% and in 1996-9 there is an addition of 5% to funds as compared to the previous year.

Borrowings Banks ceased financing MPSRTC from 1993-94. *Borrowings from IDBI have been reduced from Rs. 432 lakhs in 1992-93 to Rs. 185 lakhs in 1996-97, a reduction of 42%. Borrowings from LIC have increased from Rs. 35 lakhs in 1992-93 to Rs. 805 lakhs in 1996-97.*

Provisions and Deposits from Outsiders

The balance on this account has increased by 103% in five years.

Sundry Creditors

These constitute capital liabilities, revenue liabilities, interest on capital contribution to the State Government and interest on capital contribution to the Central Government.

Capital Liabilities

These liabilities are arising due to party-wise, year-wise details of credit purchases not having been worked out in any Division of MPSRTC. There is an increase of 88% in five years.

Revenue Liabilities

They comprise mainly interest due on loans obtained

from banks and financial institutions. There was a reduction of 50% in five years time. MPSRTC has not paid Audit Fee payable to Indian Audit & Accounts Department (Central Government) for 10 years from 1985-86 to 1994-95 aggregating Rs. 109 lakhs. This amount is included in the above balance.

Interest on Capital Contribution to State Government

There was no balance of interest on capital contribution payable to the State for two years from 1992-93 to 1993-94. In 1994-95, there was an outstanding balance of Rs. 2426 lakhs payable to the State Government and the same has increased by 32% in three years.

Interest on Capital Contribution to Central Government

There was no balance of interest on Capital Contribution payable to the Central Government for two years from 1992-93 to 1993-94. In 1994-95, the interest component payable to the Centre has increased by 117% in 1996-97.

MV Taxes

There was no dues to the State Government in respect of MV taxes in 1992-93 and 1993-94. The first year's default came up in 1994-95 which has gradually increased to Rs. 10624 lakhs in 1996-97, an increase of 126% in three years.

Salaries and Other Outstandings

This component comprises Salaries and Allowances payable to staff, besides Audit Fee payable to Indian Audit & Accounts Department. There were no outstandings for two years in 1992-93 and 1993-94. The acumulation of outstandings started in 1994-95 and has registered an increase of 93% in three years.

Revaluation Reserve Account

There is an outstanding balance of Rs.5268 lakhs in 1995-96. This is a contra entry made for Revaluation of Assets -- Land & Buildings -- in 1995-96

ASSETS

Fixed Assets

The increase of Fixed Assets in five years by 430% is not due to investments in Fixed Assets. The Revaluation of Land by Rs. 46953 lakhs (Book Value Rs.101 lakhs) and Buildings by Rs. 3418 lakhs (Book Value Rs.1619 lakhs) during 1995-96, an increase of 2800% mainly contribute to a phenomenal increase in their size.

Investments

There was a reduction of 99%. Remittances made to Central Provident Fund, Regional Provident Fund Commissioner comprising Employees' Subscription to Provident Fund and Employer's Contribution to Provident Fund have been wrongly shown as investments. This fund does not belong to MPSRTC.

Current Assets

There are six items under this heading and the significant ones are Stores, Stock and Materials (including Work-in-Progress), Advances and Deposits, and Sundry Debtors, which are dealt with hereunder:

would also hesitate to give any loan to a corporation whose revenue liabilities are of the order of Rs. 35210 Lakhs against an annual turnover of Rs. 17379 *with no positive action in sight or other workable arrangements made to clear them in the near future. MPSRTC is able to operate only two-thirds of its fleet with 794 buses off road. A third of the fleet is thus unable to generate revenues. The situation warrants settlement of liabilities and restructuring of Capital in consultation with Financial Institutions and the Central and State Govenments.*

Fleet Strength and Position of Off-Road Vehicles

Fleet strength and the percentage of buses operated and those which are off-road is a good index of the operational efficiency of a transport corporation. Accordingly a statement of Fleet Strength vs. Vehicles Off-Road for four years is given in Table 1.11.

Table 1.11

S. No.	*Year*	*Fleet Strength*	*Average age in Years*	*No. of Buses off-road*	*%*	*No. of Buses on-road*	*No. of New Buses added (Replacements)*
1.	1993-94	2737	8.17	498	18.19	2237	116
2.	1994-95	2615	8.60	448	17.51	2167	91
3.	1995-96	2565	9.30	583	22.72	1982	50
4.	1996-97	2452	9.79	794	32.38	1658	72

Source: MPSRTC's reply to Consultant's Questionnaire

It will be noticed that fleet strength has reduced from 2737 in 1993-94 to 2452 in 1996-97 or 10%. In the meantime, off-road vehicles had increased from 498 in 1993-94 to 794 in 1996-97 i.e. an increase of 59%. Total fleet strength to buses off-road has increased from 18.19% in 1993-94 to 32.38% in 1996-97. Number of buses on road in 1993-94 were 2239 while in 1996-97 it was only 1658, i.e. a reduction of 26%. This may be compared with the All-India average of vehicles held to vehicles on road which is around 90%. One-third of the fleet of MPSRTC i.e. 794 buses are off-road which means that two-thirds of the buses which are on road are being flogged. Average age of fleet was 8.17 years in 1993-94 which has risen to 9.79 years in 1996-97, an increase by 20% which shows that Corporation is incurring heavy maintenance expenditure in running overaged vehicles. As the age of vehicles increase there has to be a proper policy of replacement of buses. There is precipitious fall in replacement of buses from 1993-94 to 1995-96. The above data indicates the lack of a good Bus Replacement Policy in the Corporation. Some attempts had however been made during 1996-97 to reverse this trend which is encouraging.

SWOT ANALYSIS

A SWOT Analysis of MPSRTC has been carried out based on discussions with MPSRTC officials to ascertain the need for reform and scope of restructuring.

Strengths

(i) 25 years of experience in road transport management.

(ii) Favourable passenger tariff.

(iii) Very favourable route pattern.

(iv) Adequate infrastructural facilities to maintain and repairs buses.

(v) Chain of Bus Stations and Bus Shelters to provide services to passengers.

(vi) Professionally trained management team.

(vii) Workforce with commitment who can be further motivated.

(viii) Congenial industrial relations.

(ix) Entering of MOU (performance contract) with Government.

(x) Internal MOU entered with Depot Managers by Management whose impact is yet to be assessed.

Weaknesses

Weaknesses of MPSRTC can be classified under Organisational Policy, Financial, HRD and Customer-Orientation as follows:

Organisational

(i) Lack of modernisation and computerisation of various activities to improve productivity and reduce response time.

(ii) Less effective organisational structure.

(iii) Inadequate system to evaluate and review critical factors for success and monitor key result areas.

Policy

(i) Non-rationalisation of MV tax system to optimise the operations.

(ii) High off-road vehicle position and inadequate vehicle replacement practices.

(iii) Sub-optimal operational units, viz., sub-depots.

Financial

(i) Inadequate financial inputs to generate sufficient internal resources to meet organisational needs.

(ii) Non-release of grant/subsidy amounts towards social concessions extended at the instance of the State Government.

(iii) Borrowings from Banks and other financial institutions at high interest rates.

(iv) High carrying cost with stocks of over Rs. 4.15 crores.

HRD

(i) Inadequate training facilities to update managerial skills and provide training to staff.

(ii) Surplus unproductive supporting staff and relatively less direct productive staff (crew).

(iii) Lack of a good work cultre and professionalism.

Customer-orientation

(i) Lack of monitoring system to assess levels of customer satisfaction and the quality of service.

(ii) Lack of sound marketing strategies.

(iii) Inadequate operational service-mix.

Opportunities

Opportunities that are open to MPSRTC can be classified into growth prospects, new business, share of market and reduction of costs.

Growth Prospects

(i) Selective hiring of private buses to improve the profitability while saving on capital cost.

(ii) Replacement of all over-aged vehicles with new vehicles to ensure maximum Average Vehicle Utilisation, least cancellations, more earnings and more passenger satisfaction.

(iii) Identifying low-cost funds for above procurement.

New Business

(i) Introduction of Luxury Service and Express Service with higher tariff of plus 25% of fare or as may be feasible and considered remunerative.

(ii) Scheduling Ordinary and Express Buses to run for 350 and 500 km respectively per day to improve Average Vehicle Utilisation.

Share of Market

(i) Very favourable route system that can support organisational productivity.

(ii) Taking advantage of running all schedules in all routes without cancellation.

Reduction of Costs

(i) Identifying the areas of contracting out in respect of cleaning and maintenance of buses, ticket booking and public enquiry systems, etc., to secure passenger satisfaction.

(ii) Banning all miscellaneous expenditure except those required for emergency operations only.

(iii) Setting in motion fuel conservation process.

Threats

(i) Issue of permits to private operators on notified routes and increased competition.

(ii) Liberalisation of permit system.

(iii) Increase of illicit and clandestine operations.

(iv) Surplus unproductive staff.

(v) Organisational inefficiencies.

The organisation's accent should be on competitiveness based on its strengths, overcoming of the weaknesses, countering threats and preparing for clearly discerned and evaluated opportunities.

PERFORMANCE EVALUATION

Several RTC's in India assess their performance on the basis of ten Critical Success Factors (CSF) which are crucial for successful operations. Resource Utilisation Factors (RUF) measures built-in capacity of the Undertaking and actual passengers carried. Employee Productivity (EP) measures average out-put per employee. Since fleet sizes vary it may be appropriate to compare cost incurred as between MPSRTC and any of the zones of a large RTC which has similar number of buses. Accordingly performance of MPSRTC has been compared with a Zone of APSRTC as shown in Table 1.12.

It will be noticed from the Table 1.12 that MPSRTC is utilising only 50% of its available capacity. MPSRTC has reached only 22.32 Kms per day per employee in respect of EP which is about half that of APSRTC's which has achieved 40.00 Kms per day per employee. Fuel cost accounts for 16% of total cost. MPSRTC has reached 4.00 KMPL as against APSRTC's 5.02 KMPL and the national average of 4.50 KMPL. Tyre expenditure is 13% of total cost. MPSRTC has reached an average of 1.11 lakh Kms per tyre compared to APSRTC's 1.25 lakh Kms. In lube performance MPSRTC is just 381

Table 1.12

S. No.	Key Result	Critical Success	Unit	MPSRTC	APSRTC	Likely Factors Addl Areas Earnings if APSRTC level is achieved (Rs./Lks)
1.	Resource	Resource Utilisation Factor (RUF)	%	0.50	1.15	22259
2.	Personnel	Employee Productivity (EP)	KMs	22.32	40.00	-
3.	Fuel	Kilometres per Litre	KMPL	4.00	5.02	962
4.	Tyre	Tyre Life (TL)	Lakh/Kms	1.11	1.25	123
5.	Lubricants	Kilometres per Litre	KMPL	381	608	163
6.	Safety	Accident Rate	%	0.16	0.16	-
7.	Regularity	(i) Breakdown Rate	10000 Kms	1.20	0.29	-
		(ii) Cancellation Rate	%	56%	4.21%	150
8.	Punctuality	(i) Late Departures	%	91%	95%	-
		(ii) Late Arrivals	%	91%	95%	-
			Total		23657	-

Source: MPSRTC's reply to Consultant's Questionnaire

KMPL which is very low compared to APSRTC's 608 KMPL. The level of safety of operations is attributable to passenger safety. Accident rate for every 10000 Kms in MPSRTC is 0.16 which is the same as in APSRTC and is considered favourable in the Country. Break down rate in MPSRTC is 1.21 per 10000 Kms as against 0.29 in APSRTC. The rate of cancellation of buses in MPSRTC is 56% which is very high compared to 4.21 obtaining in APSRTC. Economic viability is getting hit on account of this factor. Late departures and late arrivals are attributable to the factor of punctuality of services. There is scope for improvement in this factor to enhance the quality of services to the travelling public.

Working Results

The corporate performance of a passenger transport undertaking can be evaluated by looking at total operations, total income and total expenditure over a period of time. The total income and total expenditure for the three years ending March 31, 97 of MPSRTC are as follows:

A. Total Income Vs Total Expenditure

Table 1.13

Rs./Lks

S. No.	*Parameter*	*1994-95*	*1995-96*	*1996-97*
1.	Total Km's run (Km's/Lks)	1911	1983	1795
2.	Total Income	15875	18119	17379
3.	Total Expenditure	9756	25662	23678
4.	Surplus/Deficit	(-)3881	(-)7543	(-)6299

Source: MPSRTC's reply to Consultant's Questionnaire

Income increased in 1995-96 by 14% while in 1996-97 it decreased by 4% when compared to 1995-96. Expenditure on the other hand increased by 30% in 1995-96 when compared to 1994-95 and decreased by 8% in 1996-97 compared to the previous year. When one looks at activity level i.e. total operations in terms of Km's in 1995-96 it is noticed that it has increased by 4% compared to previous year while activity level dropped by 9% in 1996-97 compared to the previous year. This appears to be due to non-availability of healthy fleet and non-operation of buses on some routes.

B. Operational Performance

Cost effective performance of a passenger transport undertaking can be evaluated on eight parameters which are given in the Table 1.14.

Table 1.14

Rs./Lks

S. No.	*Parameter*	*1994-95*	*1995-96*	*1996-97*	*% over 1994-95*
1.	No. of Buses held (No.)	2667	2584	2434	(-)9
2.	No. of Buses operated (No.)	2174	1941	1686	(-)22
3.	Average Fleet Utilisation (%)	82	75	69	(-)16
4.	No. of Km's run (Km's/Lks)	1911	1983	1796	(-)6
5.	Average Km's operated per bus per annum (Km's)	87907	102167	106499	12
6.	Average Km's operated per day/per Bus (Km's)	240	280	292	22
7.	Earnings per Km (Paise)	832	914	968	16
8.	Cost per Km (Paise)	1034	1294	1319	28
9.	Surplus/Deficit per Km (Paise)	(-)202	(-)380	(-)351	74

It will be seen from the data which is for three years ending 31 Mar. 97 that Average Fleet Utilisation was 82% during 1994-95, 75% during 1995-96 and has dropped to 69% during 1996-97. Off-road vehicle position has been deteriorating year after year indicating the Corporation's inability to strengthen its preventive maintenance practices. Although total KM's run had increased during 1995-96 by 4% compared to previous year it had slumped by 9% during 1996-97 showing predominance of off-road vehicles and Corporation's inability to maintain good health of its fleet. While 30% of fleet is off-road, staff complement has been maintained without any reduction resulting in unproductive labour. Average Km's operated per day has gradually increased from 240 in 1994-95 to 280 in 1995-96 registering an increase by 12% and to 293 in 1996-97 again registering an increase of 4%. Earnings per Km had also increased from 832 paise in 1994-95 to 914 paise in 1995-96 i.e. an increase of 10% and 968 paise in 1996-97 i.e. 6% over the previous year. This shows that existing resources are stretched and strained.

Cost per Km was 1034 paise in 1994-95 and had risen to 1294 paise in 1995-96 registering an increase by 25% and in 1996-97 it had touched 1319 paise registering an increase by only 2%. Expenditure during 1996-97 was thus well under check. *It is clear from the above that earnings had increased by 6% during 1996-97 compared to previous year while expenditure has been kept under check.*

C. Fleet Utilisation

A close examination of the composition and age of fleet gives the efficacy of fleet utilisation. Fleet utilisation is a function of health of buses, number of break-downs, dependence on batteries and other vital spares and preventive maintenance practices. MPSRTC had a fleet of 2434 as on 31 Mar. 97 and in Dec. 97 it had come down to 2294 which include 1206 buses with an average of 9 years. 794 buses are off-road requiring heavy repairs. Of the total 2294 buses, 6 are Deluxe buses, 832 are operated either as express buses in night operation or on Inter-state long distance routes while the rest numbering 1456 are operated as ordinary buses. Fleet Utilisation has gradually come down from 82% in 1994-95, 75% in 1995-96 and 69% in 1996-97. *This downward trend in Fleet Utilisation is ascribable to inadequate preventive maintenance practices.*

D. Workshop Performance

Evaluation of workshop performance is done by ascertaining number of various units overhauled (buses, engines, gear boxes), expenditure incurred on spares and materials, expenditure on labour, and cost per unit overhauled. It is workshop's efficiency which literally keeps vehicles moving. It is useful to review the operationality of buses and grade them for replacement. Vehicle Scrapping and Vehicle Replacement Policy has to be evolved and this has to be dovetailed with preventive maintenance practices to ensure robust health of fleet. The Table 1.15 gives the picture on these parameters.

It will be observed that Workshop Performance had deteriorated and number of Buses Overhauled was lower by 29% during 1996-97 when compared to 1994-95. During the same period, Engine overhaul had come down by 34% and Gear Box overhauling by 28%. Material consumption had registered a reduction of 2% while production on an average has come down by 20% in 1996-97 compared to 1994-95 in respect of all three products cited on labour increased by 23% while the activity came down by about 30%.

Labour productivity has thus shown a steep fall during the above period. Cost of overhauling a bus had increased in 1995-96 by 21% and by 33% in 1996-97 when compared to the previous years.

E. Equivalence Factors

As there were no ready made standards available in MPSRTC, Equivalence Units in the instant case have been worked out based on APSRTC's standards for the limited purpose of arriving at cost of overhauling of a bus (Table 1.16):

Table 1.15

S. No.	*Parameter*	*Unit*	*1994-95*	*1995-96*	*1996-97*	*% Improvement/ Decline*
1.	No. of Buses Overhauled	Nu	890	843	631	(-) 29
2.	No. of Engines Overhauled	Nu	2471	2041	1619	(-) 34
3.	No. of Gear Boxes Overhauled	Nu	4923	2453	3550	(-) 28
4.	Equivalence Units (Engines) 1 Engine = 5.0 Gear Boxes	Nu	985	491	710	(-) 28
5.	Total Engines (2+4)	Nu	3456	2532	2329	(-) 33
6.	Equivalence Units (Buses) 1 C/O Bus = 6.5 Engines	Nu	532	390	358	(-) 30
7.	Total C/O Buses (1+6)	Nu	1422	1233	989	(-) 30
8.	Expenditure on Spares/Matls.	Rs./Lak	818	819	799	2
9.	Expenditure on Labour	"	1234	1339	1519	23
10.	Total Workshop Expenditure	"	2052	2158	2318	13
11.	Average cost per Bus	Rs.	144534	175415	234121	62
12.	Percentage increase over previous year		--	21%	33%	

Source: MPSRTC's reply to Consultant's Questionnaire

Table 1.16

S. No.	*Parameter*	*Unit*	*Complete Overhaul*		
			Gear Box	*Engine*	*Bus*
1.	No. of average labour hours required	Hrs.	40	300	2200
2.	Rate per Labour Hour	Rs.	50	50	50
3.	Labour Charges	Rs.	2000	15000	110000
4.	Average Material Consumption	Rs.	6000	21000	110000
5.	Overhead Charges (100% of Labour Charges)	Rs.	2000	15000	110000
6.	Total Cost of Overhaul	Rs.	10000	51000	330000

Note: Equivalence Factor : 5 Gear Boxes = 1 Engine
6.5 Engines = 1 Bus
32.5 Gear Boxes = 1 Bus

F. Tyreshop Performance

Tyre maintenance practices have to be accorded importance as MPSRTC spends Rs. 1100 Lakhs per annum on tyres. Proper tyre maintenance practices extend the average maiden life of tyres and its retreadability factor also improves. The Tyre Shop Performance for three years ending 31st March 1997 is as shown in Table 1.17.

Productivity in Tyre Shop has fallen by 10% in 1995-96 compared to 1994-95 and by 15% in 1996-97 when compared to the earlier year. Tyre Maintenance Practices should be totally reviewed and good practice manual drawn up afresh to ensure maximum tyre life through better Retreadability Factor (i.e. more number of times retreading/recapping each tyre) besides obtaining maximum kilometres in the maiden life of tyres.

Comparison of Key Result Areas of MPSRTC with APSRTC and MSRTC

The overall efficiency of a passenger transport undertaking is evaluated through ten Key Result Areas

Table 1.17

S. No.	*Parameter*	*Unit*	*1994-95*	*1995-96*	*1996-97*
1.	No. of Tyres Retreaded/ Recapped	No.	25049	22643	19232
2.	Expenditure on Raw Materials	Rs./Lks	208	237	222
3.	Expenditure on Labour	"	12	15	15
4.	Expenditure on Overheads	"	12	15	15
5.	Total Expenditure	"	242	277	253
6.	Average cost per RT/RC	Rs.	965	1180	1314
7.	Price of one New Tyre, Tube, Flap	Rs.	6500	6800	7150
8.	Average Km's obtained from New Tyre in maiden life	Km's	45483	45171	44357
9.	Cost per Km (CPK) of New Tyres	Paise	14	15	16
10.	Average Km's obtained from RT/RC tyres (Cold Process)	Km's	28117	28241	27725
11.	...Ditto .. (Hot Process)	Km's	15316	18273	18807
12.	Total Km's obtained from RT/RC Tyres	Km's	43433	46514	46532
13.	Average Km's obtained (Cold/Hot)	Km's	21716	23257	23266

Source: MPSRTC's reply to Consultant's Questionnaire

Legend: RT = Retreading, RC = Recapping

shown in Table 1.18. The Key Result Areas of MPSRTC are compared with Andhra Pradesh State Road Transport Corporation (APSRTC) and Maharashtra State Road Transport Corporation (MSRTC). All Key Areas are worked out based on per kilometre of operation. It will be observed that in comparison with APSRTC, MPSRTC is incurring comparatively more expenditure in Key Result Areas such as Personnel, Workshop Maintenance, Stores, Lubricants, Taxes and Interest on Loans. MPSRTC appears to have around 30-35% excess

Table 1.18

Cost per Kilometre

S.No.	Key Area	MPSRTC (Rs.)	APSRTC (Rs.)	MPSRTC (Rs.)	% Increase in MPSRTC on APSRTC	Likely order of savings (Rs./Lks)
1.	Gross Earnings	9.68	9.51	9.80	02	-
2.	Gross Expenditure:					
	(i) Personnel	4.21	3.77	4.45	12	-
	(ii) Fuel	2.14	1.76	2.09*	22	962
	(iii) Tyres	0.61	0.63	0.60	(-) 3	123*
	(iv) Workshop	0.93	0.42	NA	121	1010
	(v) Stores	0.47	0.27	0.56	74	540
	(vi) Lubricants	0.24	0.11	*	118	163
	(vii) Taxes	2.10	1.39	1.59	51	600
	(viii) Interest	0.87	0.16	0.23	443	800
	(ix) Miscellaneous	1.05	0.36	0.36	193	1050
	(x) Depreciation	0.47	0.77	0.73	(-)64	16
3.	Total Gross Expenditure	13.09	9.48	10.61	38	5248
4.	Surplus/Deficit	(1-3)	(-) 3.41	0.03	(-) 0.81	

Note: Lubricants are included in Fuel in MSRTC. Workshop expenditure of MPSRTC is not available.

Source: Published Statistics of three Corporations.

Although tyre cost per Km of operation is less by 2 Paise in MPSRTC compared to APSRTC, tyre life is 13% less in the former Corporation compared to the latter. Savings on this parameter are therefore calculated on comparative tyre life. When we compare MPSRTC with APSRTC on these ten parameters it will be noticed that there is ample scope for MPSRTC to step up its efficiency in all the parameters.

staff in relation to its fleet and operations. It may be noted that APSRTC is incurring more expenditure on depreciation because of additional provision of 20% on rolling stock over and above the normal depreciation chargeable to meet price escalation in the year of replacement of bus. It may be noted that average age of fleet in APSRTC is about 4.5 years while in MPSRTC it is over 9.0 years. When MPSRTC's performance is compared with MSRTC's performance on the under mentioned KRA's it will be noted that MSRTC is incurring more expenditure on Personnel Cost and Stores compared to MPSRTC. In other parameters like Fuel, Tyres, Taxes, Interest and Miscellaneous Expenses MSRTC is better than MPSRTC. In Depreciation, MSRTC like APSRTC is making extra provision to meet price escalation in the year of replacement of buses. With regard to age of fleet MSRTC's data is not available, hence no comments.

Accumulated Losses

The following Table 1.19 indicates the accumulated losses for three years ending March 31, 97:

Table 1.19

Rs./Lakhs

S. No.	*Particulars*	*1994-95*	*1995-96*	*%*	*1996-97*	*%*
1.	Accumulated losses as at beginning of the year	18651	22532	+ 21	30075	33
2.	Loss for the year	3881	7543	+94	6299	(-)16
3.	Accumulated losses at close of year	22532	30075	+33	36374	+21

Source: MPSRTC's reply to Consultant's Questionnaire & Accounts of 1996-97

Accumulated losses in 1995-96 increased by 33% over the previous year and by 21% in 1996-97 over 1995-96. As on 31 March 97 total accumulated losses were of the order of Rs. 36374 Lakhs. Loss for the year 1995-96 had increased by 94% compared to 1994-95 and reduced in 1996-97 by 16%

compared to 1995-96. There appears to be some control on expenditure during 1996-97.

Restructuring Process

Restructuring MPSRTC involves marketing, human resource, finances, commercial, material, workshops, operations, schedules and overall organisational change management. The restructured organisation has to cope with the changing market needs, achieve the business goals and make the corporate vision a reality. Vision, mission and passion to excel must become the watchwords of a new work culture.

A strategic approach is suggested under each of the important aspects of the restructuring plan.

Marketing Restructuring:

(i) Expand capacities to service all District Headquarters and neighbouring State capital cities.

(ii) Broaden service facilities by way of Ordinary, Fast Service, Express, Luxury, Hi-Tech buses with different fare/stage structures to suit various needs and sections of the population.

(iii) Strive for customer/passenger satisfaction by improving safety, regularity and punctuality of services.

(iv) Tie up with Tourism Corporation/other public undertakings and meet their transport needs.

(v) Introduce Booking Agencies at all important traffic points.

(vi) Organise regular traffic/opinion surveys to identify profitable routes.

(vii) Conduct regular opinion survey to refine operations to secure better passenger satisfaction.

(viii) Introduction of marriage, personal, excursion tours to fill idle time of spare vehicles.

(ix) Introduction of "Transport Cards".

Financial Restructuring

(i) Identify low cost fund sources.

(ii) Reduce interest liabilities.

(iii) Conversion of State/Central Government loans as equity.

(iv) Conversion of interest due to State and Central Government as equity.

(v) Clearance of loans/interests of Finance Institutions/Banks by obtaining low cost funds.

(vi) Rationalisation of MV tax system to improve operational viability.

(vii) Waiver of MV taxes due to the State Government to set off the cost of services rendered by the Corporation by way of travel concession.

(viii) Depreciation Fund provision of Rs. 20.00 lakhs (?) may be waived.

(ix) Rationalisation of internal accounts and audit system.

(x) Obtain grants and budgeted subsidies from State Government towards bus pass concessions.

Human Resource Restructuring

(i) Lay down norms of staffing and reduce unproductive supporting staff.

(ii) Improve the employee productivity by deploying required crew.

(iii) Introduction of inter-functional transferability of supporting staff categories to Drivers/Conductors.

(iv) Payment of employees' terminal benefits.

(v) Introduction of suitable VRS and offer to all willing supporting staff.

(vi) Introduction of structured managerial and supervisory development training programmes for updating skills.

(vii) Effective implementation of MOU system.

(viii) Strengthening good employee-relation schemes.

(ix) Introduction of suitable incentive schemes for all employees.

Commercial Restructuring

(i) Leasing and renting of Corporation infrastructure.

(ii) Introduction of advertisements on bus stations, buses, bus shelters, tickets, CTV advertisement, etc.

(iii) Introduction of parcel and courier services through Corporation buses.

(iv) Maximise luggage revenues i.e. accompanied as well as unaccompanied luggage.

(v) Maximise the revenue on postal services.

(vi) Maximise the revenue on paper parcel service.

Material Management Restructuring

(i) Introduction of integrated material management systems.

(ii) Stocking of Depot spares inventory at 4 Zonal Headquarters.

(iii) Standardising stocking of spare parts with rationalised minimum and maximum limits as per the consumption pattern in order to reduce inventory carrying cost.

(iv) Rationalisation of purchase policies to reduce inventory.

(v) Rationalisation of standardisation of disposal/auction activities of vehicles, scrap, tyres, batteries, etc.

(vi) Tie up with oil companies to secure POL at reasonable rates.

Operational Restructuring

(i) Scheduling of buses with minimum inputs of bus and crew for given traffic demand and design cost-effective transport system.

(ii) Structuring of operations with optimum service mix to have better return.

(iii) Rationalisation of ticket system as per the service mix.

(iv) Standardisation of various types of services with different stage structures.

(v) Rationalisation of fare structure.

(vi) Identification of threats from competitors on each route and formulate strategies for effective encounter.

(vii) Identification of opportunities in terms of change of timings, permit variations, etc.

(viii) Strengthening of bus station management.

(ix) Strengthening of quality of services by improving safety, regularity and punctual operations.

(x) Creation of passenger relation cells.

(xi) Strengthening passenger information system.

(xii) Introduction of privately hired buses to improve profitability.

(xiii) Augmentation of services on all high density routes.

(xiv) Rescheduling of low density and vehicle utilisation services.

(xv) Introduction of services on all approved routes.

(xvi) Take advantage of route pattern as 71% routes have length of more than 100 km.

(xvii) Strengthening of all inter-state routes.

(xviii) Restructuring 20 approved routes which have overlaps ranging from 5 to 56 km.

(xix) Introduction of Hi-Tech buses to all District Headquarters with modern facilities.

Organisational Restructuring

(i) Smartsizing of Corporate Office with minimum staff. A lean Corporate Office is recommended.

(ii) Closing of all Regional and Central Workshops to reduce cost of operation on Workshop repairs.

(iii) Abolition of all Divisional and Sub-Depots to minimise the personnel cost on not very productive offices and staff.

(iv) Creation of 4 self-contained near autonomous operational Zones with appropriate delegation of powers.

(v) Establishing a strong one-tier system controlled by Zonal Office with supporting functions governed by federal administration from Corporate Office.

(vi) Grouping of homogeneous functions to bring about economy.

Management Information System Restructuring

(i) Introduction of effective management information systems.

(ii) Regular monitoring of Critical Successful Factors (CSF) to improve overall performance.

(iii) Regular and timely exchange of information on few vital areas to focus managers' attention and bring about competitive spirit.

(iv) Introduction of performance appraisal and review system.

(v) Introduction of computers.

Vehicle Maintenance Restructuring

(i) Introduction of preventive and breakdown maintenance systems.

(ii) Enforcement of sound replacement policy.

(iii) Strengthening of maintenance-operational systems and monitoring.

(iv) Creation of Zonal Maintenance Engineers for this purpose.

(v) Introduction of technical, managerial and operational controls for fuel to improve use efficiency and performance.

(vi) Introduction of technical controls in the area of tyres, lubes, batteries, springs, etc. to reduce the cost of operations.

(vii) Scrapping of all vehicles over ten years age.

(viii) Repairing of all vehicles which are less than ten years age.

(ix) Auction of 6 Eicher vehicles.

(x) Rationalisation of fleet by making Bhopal, Indore as Leyland Comet bus and Jabalpur-Raipur as Tata bus zones.

Restructuring of Workshops

(i) Abolition of all Regional Workshops and Central Workshops to reduce Workshop repair costs.

(ii) Establishment of Body Building Unit at Gwalior along with Printing Press and Training College.

(iii) Establishment of four Zonal Workshops Coterminus with Zonal operational Units along with Tyre Retreading Shop and Training Schools.

(iv) Control of Body Building Unit and Training College to be vested in Corporate Office.

(v) Modernisation of Zonal Workshop Body Building units with latest machinery.

Barriers to Restructuring Process

We have to contend with a number of barriers, such as resistance to change at all levels, organisational overload, scepticism about the process, etc. Overcoming these barriers successfully is essential to launch and sustain the restructuring efforts.

The restructuring must enable people to perceive goals clearly and their roles clearly and fit into their new roles. This would involve new responsibilities and new relationships calling for new attitudes and behavioural patterns that have to emerge spontaneously throughout the organisation. It is not merely implementing changes but consolidating and improving on them. Some of the important barriers to Corporation restructuring are:

(i) Lack of understanding/knowledge of need for restructuring.

(ii) Low credibility of management action.

(iii) "What is in it for me?" attitude.

(iv) Lack of conviction/involvement of employees.

(v) Status quo mindset and resistance to change.

(vi) Poor planning of restructuring programme.

(vii) Poor and delayed execution of restructuring plan.

(viii) Lack of focus/commitment of top management.

(ix) Lack of expertise.

(x) Inadequate Government policy support by way of legal and institutional arrangements.

Financial Assistance Sought

Financial Adviser and Chief Accounts Officer MPSRTC had furnished a statement indicating 'Financial Assistance' of Rs. 63710.00 lakhs sought by them from which the following Table 1.20 has been done derived:

Table 1.20

S. No.	*Item*	*Rs./Lakhs Amount*
1.	Liabilities due to State Govt:	
	(i) M V Taxes	16000
	(ii) Loans	2350
	(iii) Guarantee Fee	50
	(iv) Interest on Capital Contribution	3610
	(v) Sub-total	22010
2.	Due to Other Institutions:	
	(i) L I C (Loan)	805
	(ii) Bank (Loan)	1261
	(iii) Other Institutions (Interest)	360
	(iv) Banks (Interest)	3824
	(v) Sub-total	6250
3.	Accumulated Arrears to Employees	6950
4.	Proposed Liabilities:	
	(i) V R S (Sep 98)	15000
	(ii) V R S (Mar 99)	9000
	(iii) V R S (Mar 00)	2500
	(iv) Sub-total	26500
5.	Fresh Investment Proposed for Modernisation of Workshops, Printing Press and Tyreshops	2000
	Total	63710

Source: MPSRTC's reply to Consultant's Questionnaire

It may be noted that MPSRTC has not included any amount for either replacement of existing overaged buses or for procurement of new buses for augmentation of services in their request for financial assistance. It is understood that MPSRTC is separately assessing its requirement of finance for restructuring.

Suggestions on Liquidation of Outstanding Liabilities

(i) Liabilities due to State/Central Govts (Rs. 22010 Lakhs): MPSRTC could make a case for consideration of State Government for waiver of MV Taxes (Rs. 16000 Lakhs) and Guarantee Fee (Rs. 50 Lakhs). With regard to loans due to State Government aggregating Rs. 2350 Lakhs it is suggested that MPSRTC may make a case to State Government to convert loan into Equity. A similar request for conversion into Equity may be made to both Central and State governments in respect of Interest due on Capital Contribution (Rs. 3610 Lakhs).

(ii) Liabilities due to other Institutions (Rs. 6250 Lakhs):

It is suggested that MPSRTC should negotiate for one time settlement in respect of LIC Loan (Rs. 805 Lakhs) and bank loan (Rs. 1261 Lakhs). With regard to interest payable to other Institutions (Rs. 360 Lakhs) MPSRTC should negotiate for waiver. There is an interest component (Rs. 3824 Lakhs) payable to banks. It is suggested that MPSRTC may negotiate with banks for either full or part waiver.

(iii) Accumulated Arrears to Employees (Rs. 6950 Lakhs):

MPSRTC has to provide funds for this payment to boost the morale of the Employees and secure effective commitment and participation in the turn around process.

(iv) Proposed Liabilities towards VRS (Rs. 26500 Lakhs):

MPSRTC should provide funds for payment in three instalments as suggested by them i.e. Sept. '98 (Rs. 15000 Lakhs), March 99 (Rs. 9000 Lakhs) and March 2000 (Rs. 2500 Lakhs).

(v) Fresh Investment for Modernisation of Workshops, Tyre shops and Printing Press (Rs. 2000 Lakhs).

It is suggested that funds should be provided through Capital Budget for 1998-99.

An Overview of Existing Situation in MPSRTC

(i) Fare structure is reasonable. However, there is scope for further improving fare structure and increasing revenues.

(ii) MPSRTC is not fully utilising all available nationalised routes.

(iii) MPSRTC does not have either an optimal or healthy fleet strength. A large proportion of its buses are 9.5 years old.

(iv) There are too many uneconomic operating Depots.

(v) There is no proper Vehicle Replacement Policy.

(vi) Fleet Rationalisation between Leyland and Tata buses has not been done. This has led to poor maintenance and higher costs.

(vii) Corporation is continuously incurring losses for the last 7 or 8 years and experiencing cash flow problems.

(viii) Corporation owes Rs. 35210 Lakhs to State Government, Central Government, Banks, Financial Institutions, etc.

(ix) It is understood that MPSRTC is separately assessing its requirements of finance for restructuring and turn around.

(x) There is lot of unproductive manpower and surplus labour force which has to be rationalised.

(xi) There is considerable surplus labour in relation to current level of operations. The assessment of number of people who are to be declared surplus would depend on proposals for raising fleet strength, time taken for augmenting fleet strength, assessment of opportunities for growth and strategy of MPSRTC. There is however ample scope and need for strengthening MPSRTC which could absorb some surplus people with adequate retraining. Estimate should indicate unproductive staff who may not be required either now or after restructuring. They should be given VRS. There may be some productive people who may be accommodated in the 'reorganisation'. Total number of falling under VRS will depend on final assessment of persons required for minimum and maximum levels of operations.

(xii) In our view MPSRTC can be restructured and if so done can give positive results.

(xiii) MPSRTC has to clearly spell out its reorganisation proposals.

(xiv) Further detailed discussions are needed to evolve a suitable restructuring package.

(xv) For securing financial assistance for restructuring, MPSRTC should negotiate with existing Creditors/ State Govt./Central Govt. quickly and arrive at suitable settlements.

(xvi) Should identify barriers for restructuring and follow a time-bound strategy.

(xvii) Should aim at capacity building and secure external assistance for this purpose.

(xviii) Should set up an Expert Team to advise CEO of MPSRTC on a day to day basis once process of restructuring commences.

(xix) The study is based on physical and financial performance of MPSRTC for three years ending 31 March 97. MPSRTC is experimenting with reorganisation at certain levels. The impact of these changes can be partially gauged when figures of physical and financial performance for 1997-98 are made available to study and comment on their efficacy and relevance in any future proposals of restructuring.

Summary of Reorganisation Proposals

The following Table 1.21 shows the summarised version of our proposed reorganisation:

Table 1.21

	Existing		*Proposed*
(i)	Divisional Offices	:	To be abolished
(ii)	Central Workshops with Stores	:	To be abolished
(iii)	Central Stores and Purchase	:	Central Stores to be abolished Retain Central Purchase Wing [See item viii (v)]
(iv)	Regional Workshops with Stores	:	To be abolished
(v)	Divisional Workshops with Stores	:	To be abolished
(vi)	Sub-depots	:	To be abolished, attach fleet and Personnel to parent depot
(vii)	Printing Press	:	To be modernised to take up (100%) printing of Tickets, Forms, Registers etc.
(viii)	Body Building Unit	:	To be modernised to take up all types of bodies of MPSRTC New Establishments: (i) 4 Zonal Offices (ii) 4 Zonal Workshops (iii) 4 Zonal Stores Purchase (iv) 4 Tyre Shops (v) 1 Central Purchase Wing

RESTRUCTURING AND PROCESS

Restructuring process may be attempted in three phases as follows:

A. First Phase:

MPSRTC should implement those activities which do not have large financial commitments but would ensure maximisation of cash inflow consistent with available resources. The following activities may be taken up immediately:

(i) Repair expeditiously 561 off road vehicles which are between 8-9 years old. This is estimated to cost Rs. 420.75 lakhs (561 buses × Rs. 0.75 lakh).

(ii) Scrap and expeditiously dispose off 233 buses which are over 10 years old to improve liquidity position.

(iii) The Corporation should launch a 'Cost Reduction' drive. A Cost Reduction Committee should be constituted consisting of Senior Managers who should identify major areas for cost reduction and ensure time-bound action. Progress should be reviewed weekly to ensure substantial results in financial terms. Cost reduction should be considered as an on-going process to bring about cost consciousness in the organisation.

(iv) Instal immediately Speed Control Devices in all vehicles of the Corporation to control speeds at 60 KMPH for Express Services and 50 KMPH for Ordinary Services to improve fuel usage factor. The additional expenditure on this account works out to Rs. 6.88 Lakhs only (Rs. 300 × 2294 Buses).

(v) Request State and Central Governments to convert loans (Rs. 2350.00 Lakhs) and Interest (Rs. 3610.00 Lakhs) as Equity.

(vi) Request State Government to waive outstanding M V Taxes (Rs. 16000.00 Lakhs).

(vii) Request State Government to accord exemption from payment of M V Taxes on 794 off-road vehicles.

(viii) Lodge immediate claim on State Government towards services rendered to various sections of the people at the instance of the State Government and secure adjustment or payment.

(ix) Form Special Task Force headed by a competent Senior Manager of MPSRTC for realisation of all commercial revenues (e.g. rentals, advertisements, Postal Bills, Police Warrant Bills, Special Hire Bills etc.) due to the Corporation from State and Central Governments, Public Sector Undertakings etc.

(x) Four Zonal offices may be located at Bhopal, Indore, Jabalpore, and Raipur. These four workshops would be able to meet the needs of overhauling/repairing of all major assemblies and tyres in respective zones.

(xi) Abolish Central Workshop and 13 Divisional Workshops and upgrade 4 Divisional Workshops as Zonal Workshops with Tyre Retreading Shop and attached Training School.

(xii) Modernise Gwalior Workshop as Body Building Unit for fabrication of bodies on both Leyland and Tata Chassis alongwith Printing Press and Training School. Also establish a Training College for training Supervisors, Junior and Senior Managers.

(xiii) Establish four Zonal Stores and Purchase Wings to cater to full requirements of Zonal Workshops and Zonal Tyre Shops.

(xiv) Rationalise fleet by using Leyland fleet in Bhopal and Indore Zones and Tata fleet in Jabalpur and Raipur Zones.

(xv) Close down 11 Divisional Offices and 13 Sub-depots. The Divisional Offices may be transferred to respective Zonal Offices. Every Sub-depot to be attached to main/parent Depot. Personnel, rolling stock and equipment to be transferred to parent depot.

(xvi) Freeze recruitment of supporting staff for a period of five years from 1997-98 onwards.

(xvii) Recruitment to productive categories alone be taken up on need-based approved assessment.

(xviii) Ban all miscellaneous expenditure except those required for emergency operations only.

(xix) Introduce Luxury Service and Express Service with higher tariff of plus 25% of fare or as may be feasible and considered remunerative.

(xx) Schedule all Ordinary and Express buses to run for 350 and 500 Kms per day respectively to improve Average Vehicle Utilisation.

(xxi) Approach State Government to rationalise M V Tax System based on a 'Percentage of Gross Revenue' per quarter instead of on 'Per Seat Per Quarter' basis as is the prudent system in APSRTC/MSRTC/KSRTC.

(xxii) There is need to professionalise management in the Areas of Finance, Materials, Company Secretary, Production and Maintenance.

B. Second Phase:

In the second phase, following activities should be taken up:

(i) Procurement of 1206 new buses estimated at Rs. 9.50 Lakhs each (Total = Rs. 11450 Lakhs) to replace all overaged vehicles of more than 10 years age.

(ii) Identifying low cost funds for the above procurement.

(iii) Scrapping and disposing of 1206 old buses by either Tender, Auction or Tender-cum-Auction basis to generate cash inflow of Rs. 844.20 lakhs at Rs. 0.70 Lakh each.

(iv) Assess internal availability and recruit operating crew to match needs of fleet of 2294 vehicles and operating schedules.

(v) Introduce V R S for supporting staff other than drivers and conductors who may be a shortage category if the fleet is increased.

(vi) All arrears due to retired Employees may be cleared by providing required amounts from Earnings over a period of six months from the commencement of the process of restructuring.

(vii) Request IOC/BPC/HPC to conduct Seminars on fuel conservation at 4 Zonal Offices at their cost for benefit of Mechanical Staff/Supervisors/Managers as is being done by the oil companies for other Corporations.

(viii) Modernise 4 Zonal Workshops and Zonal Tyre Retreading Shops (Rs. 1500.00 Lakhs).

(ix) Modernise Body Building Unit and Printing Press (Rs. 1000.00 Lakhs).

(x) Dispose of Divisional Workshops and Central Workshop at Mhow.

(xi) Identify areas for cost reduction and implementation of action plan to reduce miscellaneous expenditure.

C. *Third Phase*

In the third phase, the following activities may be taken up:

(i) Identify excess staff in supporting categories and in Traffic Department and allow interchangeability depending upon their aptitude, qualifications, experience and suitability.

(ii) Design organisational structure to suit 3000 Schedules.

(iii) Concentrate on improving employee productivity from 22.32 Kms to 45.00 Kms per day in the first stage with the target of 50.00 km's per day in the second stage.

(iv) Clear loans of Banks and LIC aggregating Rs. 2066.00 lakhs.

(v) Computerise 57 Depots at a cost of Rs. 500.00 lakhs and training Managers, Supervisors and Staff Members with help of companies which supply hardware.

(vi) Approach government for suitable fare structure.

Acknowledgements

The Report is based on the study of data and information made available by MPSRTC and discussions held with Managing Director and other Senior and Junior level Managers at several sittings. We are of the view that MPSRTC has the potential and inherent capacity to make a quick turnaround in its performance if it is restructured along the lines suggested by us. There are however many areas which need in-depth study and analysis. Further discussions have to be held with Managing Director and Managers at all levels to enable us to elicit their views and chalk out a detailed plan of restructuring of MPSRTC alongwith the methodology and process for motivating personnel and bringing about effective changes. Such a plan should build capability to manage change and respond to the needs of the customers and ensure continued growth and progress for all stake holders. I P E places on record its gratitude to the Asian Development Bank, the Government of MP and the Managing Director of MPSRTC, Shri A V Singh and all the Managers and staff of MPSRTC for the help and cooperation extended to it.

Report on Study of MPSRTC, Bhopal

Index

Capital Structure

Under Sec. 23(1) of the RTC's Act 1950, the Central and State Governments may provide to a Corporation established by the State Government any capital that may be required by the Corporation in such proportion as may be agreed by both Governments any capital that may be required by the Corporation. The capital contribution agreed to be subscribed between State and Central Govts. at a the time of formation of MPSRTC in 1962 was in the ratio of 3:1 respectively. This ratio was subsequently revised to 2:1 during April '69. The Corporation has to pay interest at the rate of 6.25% p.a. on capital contribution to the State and Central Govts. irrespective of the fact whether the corporation made a profit or loss. In effect therefore this capital contribution was in the nature of 'preference' capital. The issue of conversion of capital contribution into "Equity" was under consideration with the Govt. of India who agreed to the representations made by the SRTC's and the decision for conversion of capital into Equity came into effect on and from 1 Apr. 96. This conversion was subject to payment of dividend on the equity at a maximum rate of 3% in the year(s) in which the Corporation makes a profit. As MPSRTC is in default of payment of interest for the last seven to eight years it has to show capital contribution and share capital separately in their Balance Sheet. The present Capital Structure of MPSRTC in respect of capital contribution and share capital is as follows (Table 1.22).

Table 1.22

Rs./Lakhs

S. No.	*Share of*	*Capital Contribution*	*Share Capital*	*Total*	*%*
1.	State Government	6545	7595	14140	78
2.	Central Government	923	3173	4096	22
3.	Total	7468	10768	18236	100

It will be noticed that share-holding between State and Centre is 8:2 respectively. MPSRTC has not been paying interest on outstanding capital contribution for the last seven or eight years. As the Corporation has not made profit for the last 7 years the question of payment of dividend on equity at

3% p.a. did not arise. Total of capital structure can be taken as equity capital for the purpose of evaluating MPSRTC's performance in the context of Debt Equity ratio. The following Table 1.23 is the break-up of debt as on 31 March 97:

Table 1.23

S. No.	*Term Loan from*	*Rs./Lakhs*	*Total*
A.	Banks:		
(i)	Punjab National Bank	389	
(ii)	State Bank of India	457	
(iii)	Allahabad Bank	83	
(iv)	State Bank of Bikaner & Jaipur	147	
(v)	IDBI	185	
(vi)	Sub-total	1261	
B.	Others:		
	LIC	805	
C.	Total		2066

Debt Equity Ratio = Equity: Debt
= 18236 : 2066
or say 1 : 0.11

As a commercial practice MPSRTC can go in for a long term loan to the extent of twice the equity i.e. upto a limit of Rs. 36572 Lakhs against an equity base of Rs. 18236 Lakhs. But they are unable to take advantage as their Balance Sheet is not healthy. Moreover they have not been able to defray several payments aggregating Rs. 35210 lakhs for the last six or seven years to Govt., banks and others as can be noticed from the following Table 1.24.

Because of the heavy liabilities which have not been settled, MPSRTC is not able to raise fresh loans. Banks or Financial Institutions would also hesitate to give any loan to a oration whose revenue liabilities are of the order of Rs. 35210

Table 1.24.

		Rs./Lakhs	
1.	Liabilities due to State Govt:		
	(i) M V Taxes	16000	
	(ii) Loans	2350	
	(iii) Guarantee Fee	50	
	(iv) Interest on capital contribution	3610	
	(v) Sub-total	22010	
2.	Dues to Other Institutions:		
	(i) LIC (Loan)	805	
	(ii) Bank (Loan)	1261	
	(iii) Other Institutions (Interest)	360	
	(iv) Bank Interest	3824	
	(v) Sub-total	6250	
3.	Accumulated Arrears of dues to Employees	6950	
4.	Total		35210

Lakhs against an annual turnover of Rs. 17379 Lakhs with no positive avenues in sight or other arrangements made to clear them in the near future. MPSRTC is able to operate only two-thirds of its fleet with 794 buses off-road. A third of the fleet is thus unable to generate revenues. The situation warrants settlement of liabilities and restructuring of Capital in consultation with Financial Institutions and the Central and State Governments.

Restructuring Process -- Phases

The restructuring of MPSRTC is based on decentralised functioning of four Zonal Units with requisite maintenance support. The Corporate Office will be the supervisory and monitoring body. The proposed scheme of reorganisation will help make the zonal units function efficiently and competitively. These units could later become independent companies or subsidiaries of a holding company. This scheme would have to be carefully worked out taking into account legal, financial, personnel, operational, maintenance, and other relevant factors. This may facilitate future efforts at disinvestment or privatisation. Restructuring process may be attempted in three phases as follows:

A. First Phase

MPSRTC should implement those activities which do not have large financial commitments but would ensure maximisation of cash in flow consistent with available resources. The following activities may be taken up immediately:

(i) The Corporation should launch a Cost Reduction Drive and constitute a Cost Reduction Committee consisting of Senior Managers who should identify major areas for cost reduction and ensure time-bound action. Progress should be reviewed weekly to ensure substantial results in financial terms. Cost reduction should be considered as an on going process to bring about cost-consciousness in the organisation.

(ii) Repair expeditiously 561 off-road vehicles which are between 8-9 years old. This is estimated to cost Rs. 420.75 lakhs (561 buses × Rs. 075 Lakh).

(iii) Scrap and expeditiously dispose of 233 buses which are over 10 years old to improve liquidity position.

(iv) Request State and Central Governments to convert loans Rs. 2350 lakhs) and interest (Rs. 3610 lakhs) as equity.

(v) Request State Government to waive outstanding MV taxes (Rs. 16000 lakhs).

Request State Government to accord exemption from payment of MV Taxes on 794 off-road vehicles.

Lodge immediate claim on State Government towards services rendered to various sections of the people at the instance of the State Government and secure adjustment or payment.

Form Special Task Force headed by a competent Senior Manager of MPSRTC for realisation of all commercial revenues (e.g. rentals, advertisements, postal bills, police warrant bills, special hire bills, etc.) due to the Corporation from the State and Central Governments, Public Sector Undertakings, etc.

Instal immediately Speed Control Devices in all vehicles of the Corporation to control speeds at 60 kmph for Express Services and 50 KMP for Ordinary Services to improve fuel usage factor. The additional expenditure on this account works out to Rs. 6.88 lakhs only (Rs. 300 × 2294 buses).

Four Zonal Offices may be located at Bhopal, Indore, Jabalpur and Raipur. These four workshops would be able to meet the needs of overhauling/repairing of all major assemblies and tyres in the respective Zones.

Abolish Central Workshop and 13 Divisional Workshops and upgrade 4 Divisional Workshops as Zonal Workshops with Tyre Retreading Shop and attached Training School. Modernising Gwalior Workshop as Body Building Unit for fabrication of bodies on both Leyland and Tata chassis along with Printing Press and Training School. Also establish a Training College for training Supervisors, Junior and Senior Managers.

Establish four Zonal Stores and Purchase Wings to cater to full requirements of Zonal Workshops and Zonal Tyre Shops.

Rationalise fleet by using Leyland fleet in Bhopal and Indore Zones and Tata fleet in Jabalpur and Raipur Zones.

Close down 11 Divisional Offices and 13 Sub-Depots. The Divisional Offices may be transferred to respective Zonal Offices. Every Sub-Depot to be attached to main/parent Depot. Personnel, rolling stock and equipment to be transferred to Parent Depot.

Freezing of recruitment of supporting staff for a period of five years from 1997-98 onwards.

Recruitment to productive categories alone to be taken up on need-based approved assessment.

Banning all miscellaneous expenditure except those required for emergency operations only.

Introduction of Luxury Service and Express Service with higher tariff of plus 25% of fare or as may be feasible and considered remunerative.

Scheduling all Ordinary and Express buses to run for 35 km and 500 km per day respectively to improve Average Vehicle Utilisation per day.

Approaching State Government to rationalise MV Tax System by collection based on a Percentage of Gross Revenue per quarter instead of on per Seat per Quarter basis as is obtaining in APSRTC/MSRTC/KSRTC.

B. Second Phase

In the Second Phase, the following activities should be taken up:

(i) Procurement of 1206 new buses at Rs. 9.50 lakhs each (Total = Rs. 11450 lakhs) to replace all over-aged vehicles more than 10 years old.

(ii) Identifying low cost funds for the above procurement.

(iii) Scrapping and disposing of 1206 old buses by either Tender? Auction or Tender-cum-Auction basis to generate cash inflow of Rs. 844.20 lakhs at Rs. 0.70 lakh each.

(iv) Recruiting balance of operataing crew to match aggregating crew for 2294 vehicles.

(v) Introducing VRS for supporting staff other than drivers and conductors.

(vi) Modernisation of Body Building Unit and Printing Press (Rs. 1000 lakhs).

(vii) Disposal of Divisional Workshops and Central Workshops at Mhow.

(viii) Identifying cost reduction areas and implementation of action plan to reduce miscellaneous expenditure.

(ix) For fuel conservation process, request IOC/BPC/HPC to conduct seminars at four Zonal Offices at their cost on fuel conservation for benefit of Mechanical Staff/Supervisors/Managers, as was done by the oil companies in other Corporations.

(x) All arrears due to retired employees have to be cleared by provisioning required amounts from Earnings over a period of six months from the commencement of the restructuring process.

C. Third Phase

In the third phase, the following activities may be taken up:

(i) Identifying excess staff in supporting categories and in Traffic Department and allowing interchangeability depending upon their aptitude, qualifications, experience and suitability.

(ii) Designing organisation's size to suit 3000 Schedules.

(iii) Concentrating on improving employee productivity from 22.32 km to 45 km per day in the first stage, with an eye on 50 km per day in the second stage.

(iv) Clearing of loans of banks and LIC aggregating Rs. 2066 lakhs.

(v) Computerisation of 57 Depots at a cost of Rs. 500 lakhs and Training Managers, Supervisors and Staff Members without extra expenditure through companies which would supply hardware.

(vi) Approaching Government for suitable fare structure based on Cost-Fare Gap Analysis.

Summary of Reorganisation Proposals

The following is the summarised version of our proposed reorganisation:

Summary of Reorganisation Proposals

Existing	*Proposed*
Divisional Offices	— To be abolished
Central Workshops with Stores	— To be abolished
Central Stores and Purchase	— Central Stores to be abolished, retain Central Purchase Wing [See Item viii(v)]
Regional Workshops with Stores	— To be abolished
Divisional Workshops with Stores	— To be abolished
Sub-Depots	— To be abolished, attach fleet and personnel to parent depot
Printing Press	— To be modernised to take up 100% printing of tickets, forms, registers, etc.
Body Building Unit	— To be modernised to take up construction of all types of bodies of MPSRTC
	New Establishments: (i) 4 Zonal Offices (ii) 4 Zonal Workshops (iii) 4 Zonal Stores/Purchase (iv) 4 Tyre Shops (v) 1 Central Purchase Wing

Acknowledgements

This report is based on the study of data and information made available by MPSRTC and discussions held with the Managing Director and other Senior and Junior-level Managers at several sittings. We are of the view that MPSRTC has the potential and inherent capacity to make a quick turn around in its performance if it is restructured along the lines suggested by us. There are, however, many areas which need in-depth study and analysis. Further discussions have to be held with the Managing Director and Managers at all levels to enable us to elicit their views and chalk out a detailed plan of restructuring of MPSRTC along with the methodology and process for motivating personnel and bringing about effective changes. Such a plan should provide for an Expert Team which can help build capacity to manage change, respond to the needs of the customers, and ensure continued growth and progress for all stakeholders.

2

Madhya Pradesh Financial Corporation — (MPFC)

The Government of MP formed a financial corporation called Madhya Pradesh Financial Corporation (MPFC) during 1955-56 under Section 3(1) of the State Financial Corporation's Act, 1951 to promote and finance small-scale industry and smaller medium industry in collaboration with the Industrial Development Bank of India (IDBI). MPFC functions on the lines of similar State Financial Corporations formed in other States in India. The working of the Corporation is governed by MPFC Standing Orders framed under SFC's Act, 1951.

Data for Report

The data required for this report was based on primary and secondary sources of information. Secondary sources include annual reports of MPFC and other published sources. The primary data was collected by administering questions to MPFC mainly to get some key information not available in published sources. The report on MPFC is based on published data and information provided by MPFC.

Industrial Environment in Madhya Pradesh

Madhya Pradesh is the largest State in the country with vast mineral wealth and forest resources. MP is self-sufficient in the production of foodgrains. 80% of the population is engaged in agriculture. Madhya Pradesh does not have a sound industrial base. 36 districts out of 45 districts of MP are industrially backward. The State Government has identified 16 growth centres whose development is expected to accelerate industrial growth. Of these, four growth centres have developed as planned.

The reasons for sluggish industrial growth are not far to seek. They include:

(i) Lack of infrastructure facilities (communication, power, transport, roads and railways).

(ii) Absence of entrepreneurship and requisite skills in the State. Existing entrepreneurs are mostly from outside the State of MP.

(iii) Inadequate investment, poor skill development and lack of proper environment to spur infrastructural and entrepreneurial development.

The Government of India announced its New Economic Policy in July 1991 with an accent on marketisation of the Indian economy. The economic reforms provide for deregulation of industry, withdrawal of controls, and a bigger role for the private sector. The State-owned public sector undertakings have to cope with the changed situation and function in an increasingly competitive situation. PSUs have to be restructured both structurally and financially, and develop competence and customer confidence to remain commercially viable, perform the assigned roles and achieve their objectives in a competitive environment. MPFC is in the process of such adjustments and the throes of change management.

MPFC is managed by a Board of Directors whose Chairman is the Finance Secretary, Government of MP. The Managing Director, a member of the Indian Administrative Service belonging to the MP cadre, is the Chief Executive of the Corporation. The MD is assisted by two General Managers and three Deputy General Managers located at the Corporate

Office at Indore. Zonal Managers in Zones and Regional Managers in Regions head their respective offices and report directly to the MD, Branch Managers in charge of Branches report to the Regional Managers.

MPFC has been set up as a Statutory Corporation to serve a socially relevant objective, i.e. as a Regional Development Bank for accelerataing the industrial growth in Madhya Pradesh, to provide financial assistance mainly to small industries and smaller of the medium-scale industries. MPFC has to raise finances and lend to industrial units at reasonable and competitive rates while maintaining profitability all through so that its own corporate growth is ensured and objectives achieved.

IDBI categorises SFCs into A, B or C categories based on recovery percentage, default to outstandings ratio, percentage of non-performing assets (NPA) and conduct of refinance account of SFCs with IDBI and Small Industries Development Bank of India (SIDBI). IDBI's criteria for classification of SFCs into A, B or C categories is at Annexure 4. IDBI's criteria for classification of assets of SFCs is at Annexure 5. MPFC falls in B category by IDBI classification which restricts its lending to Rs. 60 lakhs. MPFC was maintaining accounts under mercantile system of accounting till March 31, 1990 from when onwards it switched over a cash system of accounting. Due to poor recoveries, MPFC faced problems of cash flow, timely repayments and availment of refinance facilities. As the cost of raising money by MPFC was high but loans were sanctioned at reasonable rates with long loan repayment periods, the interest spread was very low. Mismatches between assets and liabilities, NPA stipulations and poor recoveries have led to losses.

Competitive Environment

MPFC is in a highly competitive environment when compared to the situation obtaining in the seventies and eighties. In future, competition will be tougher. IDBI set up the Small Industries Development Bank of India (SIDBI) to take over its erstwhile commitments to SFCs and financing of small-scale industry. SIDBI, which is now the refinancier of MPFC, is introducing new financial schemes at competitive rates of interest to compete with banks and other financial institutions in the private sector. In this milieu of competitive environment and universal banking, it may be difficult for MPFC or other SFCs to survive, grow and make profits for future growth unless they become efficient and both quality product and customer service conscious. A Committee has been constituted with Mr. S.H. Khan, then Chairman, IDBI, to examine the present status and future role of SFCs while Government of India have appointed a Committee under the Chairmanship of Mr. M. Narasimham, a former Governor of the Reserve Bank of India to examine the role of the banking sector in the context of economic reforms. The role of SFCs also under scrutiny. These reports are under review by the Government. Pending decisions of the Government on these reports, MPFC should radically improve its performance and viability to be able to cope with the changes and survive in the present competitive environment and ensure steady growth.

Capital Structure

The SFCs were promoted by the Industrial Development Bank of India (IDBI) and the respective State Governments. The capital structure of the Corporation is furnished in the Table 2.1. The share of capital contribution between MP State and IDBI was 50:50 till March 31, 1990. The present ratio of share capital between the State and IDBI is 2:1. The total paid-up capital on March 31, 1997 was Rs. 8495 lakhs, including IDBI's share and share of other banks/LIC, etc., as under potential and industry performance, obtain progress reports from assisted units and organise periodical inspections of assisted units by technical staff. MPFC should, however, resist the temptation to extend its network and set up too many branches with too little business and uneconomic operations. Its out reach is more important than the number of branches. MPFC should develop the concept of Partnerships, Alliances

Table 2.1
Capital Structure of MPFC for the year 1996-97

(Rs. in lakhs)

S. No.	*Share Capital*		*Total*
A.	Ordinary capital [u/s 6(1)]:		
(i)	State Government		5469
(ii)	IDBI		2403
(iii)	Others:		
	- Scheduled Banks	24	
	- LIC/Banks/Individuals/Others	3	27
	Total		7899
B.	Special Capital [u/s 4(A)]:		
(i)	State Government		125
(ii)	IDBI		125
	Total		250
C.	Loan in lieu of Share Capital:		
(i)	State Government		173
(ii)	IDBI		173
	Total		346
D.	Grand Total		8495

Source: Annual Report for 1996-97

and Linkages (PAL) and a consortium approach so that risk is shared and growth ensured.

Portfolio Revamp

MPFC should concentrate on sunrise and service sector industries which are gaining importance in India and will be a growth sector in the global market of the 21st century. This will help minimise risks associated with recovery of principal and interest. MPFC should also increase fee-based income. MPFC should procure low-cost, long-term funds and concentrate on giving medium-term loans to secure good interest spread and better match assets and liabilities rather than giving long-term loans to borrowers with thin margins. MPFC should resort to consortium lending along with other interested and suitable financial institutions, including commercial banks, MPIDC, LIC, etc., to spread the risk. MPFC would have to become a lean organisation to improve personnel productivity.

Consolidation of Business

The existing delegation of powers needs to be enhanced to secure decentralised decision-making. MPFC should rope in SIDBI and banks, etc., as strategic partners in their business and aim at diversification in a big way to suit the requirements of all types and sizes of business within the ambit of their objectives.

Streamlining of Operations

MPFC should streamline operations by ensuring prompt recoveries from the existing borrowers and strengthen the appraisal systems for prospective borrowers. MPFC should also resort to 'one-time settlement' (OS) wherever it is found expedient. MPFC should take cases of defaulting borrowers to the Debt Recovery Tribunal (DRT) for recovery or settlement. To improve operations in any organisation, professionalism is a necessity. MPFC should concentrate on professionalisation of management. A Voluntary Retirement Scheme (VRS) should be introduced to weed out surplus and unproductive staff. Employees whose productivity is below the standard and who are unlikely to improve either on account of lack of professional qualification or age should be identified and VRS offered. Wherever branches and other offices of MPFC are functioning ineffectively and unprofitably, they should be closed down, staff adjusted or given VRS and assets transferred to the nearby Branch/Region. MPFC should consciously position itself as a vibrant financial institution by providing wide publicity through magazines, journals, newspapers, TV, etc. Latest schemes offered by other financial institutions in the private sector must be studied along with requirements of small-scale industries in MP and devise new and appropriate schemes and act as a catalyst for quick growth of the small-scale sector. Special Task Forces should be established with specific tasks of watching recoveries, monitoring of performance of projects and watch progress of cases referred to Debt Recovery Cell.

Age of Overdues

Of the total dues of Rs. 13968 lakhs outstanding as on March 31, 1997, amount outstandng for over three years and above is Rs. 11707 lakhs or 87% as seen in Table 2.2.

Table 2.2
Age of Overdues

(Rs. in Lakhs)

S. No.	*Age of Overdues*	*Amount*		
		Principal	*Interest*	*Total*
1.	Upto 1 year	238	57	295
2.	1 to 3 years	873	541	1414
3.	3 years and above	9025	2682	11707
4.	Legal cases (suit filed)	533	119	552
	Total	10669	3299	13968

Source: MPFC's Annual Report for 1996-97

The aggregate of dues of three years and above and legal cases (suits filed) is Rs. 12258 lakhs. The break-up between 3-6 years and above 6 years is given in Table 2.3.

Table 2.3
Outstanding Period of Overdues

Period of outstanding	*Rs. in Lakhs*
3 to 6 years	5543
Above 6 years	6715
Total	12258

Change in Accounting System

MPFC has been maintaining accounts under 'mercantile system' (accrual basis) of accounting till March 31, 1990. From

April 1, 1990 it switched over to 'cash system' of accounting in respect of income while maintaining mercantile system in respect of expenditure, as per stipulation of RBI.

Review by Committees

MPFC has constituted Review Committes at Zonal Offices and Corporate Office called as Zonal Review Committee and Head Office Default Review Committee to review cases and pressurise defaulters for remittance of overdues. The progress made by this mechanism can be seen from the data given in Table 2.4 which is encouraging.

Table 2.4

Progress of Disposal by Review Committees

S. No.	*Review of Committee*	*No. of Cases*
1.	Cases of disposal of taken-over assets	273
2.	Review of cases by Zonal Committees	61
3.	Review of Cases by Head Office Default Review Committee	236
4.	Review of Cases for Revival Packages	13
5.	Cases of condonation of delays and allowing of rebates	16
6.	Cases fit for legal action	232
7.	Total cases reviewed by Committees	831

Source: Annual Report of MPFC for 1996-97

Taken-over Units and Sale of Assets

MPFC took over 266 units for disposal as on April 1, 1996, while another 158 units were taken over during 1997-98, totalling 424 units. Of these, 66 units were slated for return to borrowers on receiving part payment against dues. Of the balance 358 units, 175 units were marked for sale, which included 21 partly sold units. MPFC had as on March 31, 1997, 205 units (including 21 units partly sold) for disposal involving an outstanding principal of Rs. 3613 lakhs and outstanding interest of Rs. 2817 lakhs, aggregating Rs. 6430 lakhs.

Settlement of Cases

Between 1992-93 and 1996-97 (five years), the Corporation settled in all 813 cases with an outstanding principal of Rs. 6560 lakhs and interest accrued of Rs. 5472 lakhs (total Rs. 12032 lakhs). In the process of one-time settlement (OTS), the Corporation had settled cases involving Rs. 7244 lakhs, i.e. 60% of the outstanding amount. Of this, it was able to recover Rs. 5215 lakhs, leaving Rs. 2029 lakhs yet to be collected. The balance of recovery of settled amount works out to 28%. There is abundant scope for MPFC to improve on the recovery front.

Recovery

MPFC has introduced a Recovery Reward Scheme (RRS) for its employees with a view to improving recovery in loan accounts classified as 'NPA' and the recovery performance is quite encouraging, as could be seen from Table 2.5.

Table 2.5
Recovery Performance in NPA Accounts

(Rs. in Lakhs)

Year	*Outstanding in NPA Accounts*	*Recovered*	*Percentage of Recovery*
1993-94	33057	4173	13
1994-95	33507	5132	15
1995-96	34301	5162	15
1996-97	33957	5465	16

As a result of better recovery in 'doubtful category', the provision of Rs. 8040 lakhs in 1995-96 for NPA has been reduced to Rs. 7716 lakhs during 1996-97. The surplus provision of Rs. 324 lakhs has, therefore, been written back to Profit and Loss Account as income during 1996-97, consequent upon which the Corporation made a net profit of Rs.434 lakhs, as otherwise Net Profit would have been marginal at Rs. 110 (434-324) lakhs.

Financing of Industries in Backward Areas

MPFC has extended financial assistance which was by and large availed by borrowers setting up industries in backward districts of the State. A majority of these loans were given to small-scale industry in general. Of the total assistance sanctioned by MPFC 86% pertains to industries in backward districts including 'no industry district' and 67% of total sanctions relate to the small-scale sector in backward districts as seen from Annexure. Average sanction per application was Rs. 11803 in backward districts and Rs. 7036 in other districts, while combined sanctions per application was Rs. 9836 per application. Average disbursement per application works out to Rs. 10932 in backward districts and Rs. 6428 in other districts, while combined average assistance was Rs. 9062 per application.

Assistance Sanctioned and Disbursed by Select SFCs

The volume of sanctions and disbursements was the lowest in the case of MPFC compared to Andhra Pradesh, Maharashtra and Karnataka over the three years ending March 31, 1997 at Rs. 9230 lakhs and Rs. 6820 lakhs respectively. Considering the size of the State and population there is ample scope for MPFC to grow.

Per Capita Assistance Sanctioned and Disbursed

The per capita assistance sanctioned and disbursed during 1996-97 turned out to be the lowest at Rs. 12.6 and Rs. 9.3 respectively. The highest was achieved by Karnataka both in respect of sanctions and disbursements in the same year at Rs. 131.2 and Rs. 113.1 respectively.

Loans Sanctioned at Various Levels

Table 2.6 provides details about the loans sanctioned at the various levels. 12% of applications were sanctioned by the Board covering 49% of the amount sanctioned. The average amount per application works out to Rs. 89 lakhs, While Head Office Loan Committee sanctioned 9% of applications involving only 8% of amount sanctioned (averaging Rs. 20 lakhs per application), Zonal Committees sanctioned 66% of applications for 17% amount (averaging to Rs. 6 lakhs per application). Managaing Director (MD) is the sanctioning authority for all new schemes, such as Asset Credit Scheme, Short-term Loans, Hire Purchase, Portfolio Management, etc. 41 applications were sanctioned by MD aggregating Rs. 2491 lakhs or Rs. 61 lakhs per application.

Table 2.6

S. No.	*Sanctioning Authority*	*Applications Sanctioned*		*Amount Sanctioned*		*Average Amount per Application*
		No.	*%*	*No.*	*%*	*(Rs. in Lakhs)*
A.	Term Loan:					
(i)	Board of Directors	37	12	3289	49	89
(ii)	Executive Committee (including Working Capital Management Term Loan)	40	13	1700	26	43
(iii)	Head Office Loan Committee	26	9	525	8	20
(iv)	Zonal Committee	201	66	1148	17	6
	Total	304	100	6662	100	22
B.	New Schemes Sanctioned by MD:					
(i)	Asset Credit Scheme	19	46	806	32	42
(ii)	Short-term Loan	14	34	510	21	36
(iii)	Hire Purchase/Portfolio Management	8	20	1175	47	147
	Total	41	100	2491	100	61
C.	Grand Total	345		9153		27

Source: Annual Report of MPFC for 1996-97

Earlier Efforts of Reorganisation

Keeping in view the state of affairs of MPFC, IDBI had asked M/s. A.F. Ferguson & Co., of Bombay to study and recommend reorganisation. M/s. Ferguson & Co., had accordingly carried out a study and submitted a report in November 1994 emphasising the need for better management of MPFC. M/s. Ferguson & Co. had also projected 'estimates/targets' for three years from 1994-95 to 1996-97 for improved performance of MPFC. The targets fixed were, however, easy of achievement and were also achieved, as could be seen from the data given in Table 2.7.

Table 2.7
Estimates/Targets fixed by Ferguson & Co., and Actual Achievements

(Rs. in Lakhs)

S. No.	*Year*	*Estimates/Targets*	*Actuals*	*Variance*
A.	Disbursements			
(i)	1994-95	2970	3988	+ 1018
(ii)	1995-96	3267	5908	+ 2644
(iii)	1996-97	3594	6628	+ 3034
B.	Recovery			
(i)	1994-95	5972	7834	+ 1862
(ii)	1995-96	6254	8964	+ 2604
(iii)	1996-97	6977	8858	+ 2671

Source: (i) Ferguson's Report (Nov. 1994)

(ii) Annual Reports for 1995-96 and 1996-97 (Recovery Performance)

(iii) MPFC's Proposal for Financial Restructuring (June 1997)

Some Conclusions from Ferguson's Report regarding Reasons for Poor Performance and Incidence of Heavy Liabilities

As the recovery of principal and interest from borrowers is in arrears, MPFC is not able to meet its disbursements fully and has to resort to issue of Bonds/Debentures thereby increasing their debt burden. In the process, it is caught in a vicious circle and is unable to service the debt. At present the main liabilities causing a heavy incidence of financial burden on MPFC are as depicted in Table 2.8.

Table 2.8
Incidence of Heavy Liabilities

(Rs. in Lakhs)

S. No.	*Burdensome Liabilities*	*Amount*	*Total*
A.	Borrowings:		
(i)	IDBI	1819	
(ii)	SIDBI	6795	
(iii)	NDI (SIDBI)	215	
	Total		8829
B.	Other Liabilities:		
(i)	Bank Overdraft	61	
(ii)	Staff Provident Fund	1	
(iii)	Unclaimed/Unpaid Dividend	2469	
(iv)	Sundry Deposits & Others	117	
(v)	Sundry Liabilities	48	
	Total		2696
C.	Long-term Bonds/Debentures		22755
D.	Grand Total		34280

Source: MPFC's Annual Report for 1996-97

Financial Difficulties

The Corporation has been passing through a phase of liquidity crisis, stagnation in business growth, and is loaded with a significant magnitude of non-performing assets. The financial difficulties faced by MPFC have been focused on from three different angles, as under:

1. Cash Flows

MPFC has been facing shortage of funds because of curtailment of traditional resource support - refinance by IDBI/SIDBI. The payment outgo in respect of refinance has been more than refinance receipts leading to liquidity crisis as could be seen from the Table 2.9.

Table 2.9

Particulars	*1993-94*	*1994-95*	*1995-96*	*1996-97**	*1997-98**
Refinance available	2000	2000	1923	-	-
Total payment to IDBI	4686	4566	3724	-	-
Payments over and above receipts	-2686	-2566	-1801	-	-
Percentage of payments over and above receipts	134	128	94	-	-

*Refinance stopped by IDBI/SIDBI pending restructuring of MPFC.

Source: MPFC's reply to Consultant's Questionnaire.

The Corporation has to borrow more to pay old borrowings and the situation pushed MPFC into a debt trap of high interest borrowings to replace old ones. In effect, therefore, borrowings were made not for improving business of the Corporation but for repayment of overdue loans. The recovery as a consequence of poor quality of loan portfolio is just not enough to meet payment obligations and, therefore, MPFC had to default in payment of either principal or interest. The disbursement level has reached a point of stagnation leaving no chance for growth.

2. Profit and Loss Account

MPFC is having accumulated losses to the extent of Rs. 11400 lakhs as on March 31, 1997. Operating profit is not possible due to poor interest recovery and high interest burden. MPFC cannot afford higher rate market borrowing even on a short-term basis. The normal interest spread is very low.

3. Balance Sheet

The Balance Sheet of MPFC is not that clean as to permit it to go for alternative sources of funding or to go in for a public issue. Besides its credit rating is poor and has defaulted in repayment of principal and payment of interest to IDBI/SIDBI.

Impact of Central Pay Scales

The Chief Minister of MP has announced that central pay scales will be made applicable to the employees of the State. It is not known whether this will be extended to MPFC. If so, the decision will result in increase of personnel cost by about 20 to 25%.

Loan Operations

The percentage of disbursement to sanctions is ranging between 65% and 87% in the five years ending March 31, 1997. When outstanding principal amount and recovery are compared, it is noticed (Table 2.10) that MPFC has been able to recover 19 to 33% of outstanding principal. There is ample scope for improvement of recovery of principal from borrowers through concerted efforts at all levels.

Table 2.10
Principal Amount Due and Recovery Made

(Rs. in Lakhs)

Year	*Amount*		*Percentage of Distribution to Sanctions*	*Principal Amount Due*	*Amount Recovered (Principal)*	*Percentage of Recovery to Amount*
	Sanctioned	*Disbursed*				
1992-93	5226	4546	87	13419	3283	24
1993-94	5293	4302	81	14689	2728	19
1994-95	5516	3988	72	16009	3751	23
1995-96	9110	5908	65	16068	4380	27
1996-97	9153	6628	72	16021	5352	33

Personnel Cost and Personnel Productivity

It will be noticed from the following Table 2.11 that Personnel Cost for handling applications has been increasing during the last five years. During the same period, applications sanctioned have reduced from 415 in 1993-94 to 368 in 1994-95, a drop of 13%. As revealed by Table, Average Personnel cost per application, which was Rs. 49753 in 1992-93, had increased to Rs. 125513 in 1996-97 while applications sanctioned have not increased in the same proportion. There is ample scope for improving business promotion activity and productivity of existing staff.

Table 2.11
Personnel Productivity

Year	*No. of Applications*	*Personnel Cost (Rs. in lakhs)*	*Personnel Cost per Application (Rs.)*	*Percentage Increase Over Previous Year*
1992-93	385	191.55	49753	-
1993-94	415	238.86	57557	16
1994-95	368	257.60	70000	22
1995-96	401	319.22	79606	14
1996-97	345	433.02	125513	58

Source: Annual Report of MPFC from 1993-94 to 1996-97

Note: Personnel Cost includes Salaries, Allowances, Employer's Contribution to PF, Gratuity Fund, Group Insurance, etc., of managers, supervisors and staff (excluding MD's salary and allowances.)

Industry-wise Loan Disbursement

It will be noticed that MPFC has so far disbursed Rs. 63267 lakhs for a variety of industries, including food, fertilizers, cement, paper, rubber products, industrial chemicals, machinery, hotel, road transport, electricity generation and supplies, plastics, gas, steam, etc. The largest share of Rs. 6584 lakhs has gone to chemical and chemical products, accounting for 10.41% of total loans sanctioned. Basic metal industries, food products follow closely. Other miscellaneous industries covering plastic, electricity, gas and steam have garnered a substantial portion of Rs. 17954 lakhs or 28.38. The above sectors account for almost 60% of the loans sanctioned.

Sources and Uses of Funds

From the statement of regrouped Sources and Uses of Funds — it is noticed that recovery of term loan (principal) and recovery of interest from borrowers was much higher in all the five years compared to disbursements (Term Loans). Besides, MPFC has been borrowing by way of IDBI (Refinance), loan from RBI, and by issuing of Bonds/Debentures and using these funds together with difference between recovery (Principal and Interest) and disbursements to meet repayment of IDBI/SIDBI, banks/RBI besides meeting financial charges (interest on borrowings) and administrative expenses. Repayments to IDBI/SIDBI have been stopped. As the position is more or less the same pattern in respect of all the above five years the figures of 1996-97 have been taken for analysis, which is presented in Table 2.12.

Table 2.12
Sources and Uses of Funds for the year 1996-97

(Rs. in Lakhs)

Particulars	*Amount*	*Total*
Opening Balance		1864
Add Recovery of Term Loans (Principal)	5352	
Add Recovery of Interest	4297	9649
Sub-total		11513
Less Disbursements (Term Loans)		5448
Add Borrowings		1969
Sub-total		8034
Less Repayments to Banks/RBI/Bonds	2123	
Repayment of Loan to IDBI/SIDBI	1	
Interest and Financial Charges	2780	
Administrative Expenses	1309	
Sub-total		6213
Closing Cash/Bank Balances		1821

Source: MPFC's Annual Report for 1996-97

Mismatch in Sources and Uses of Funds

It will be noticed from Table 2.13 given that the recoveries, including Principal and interest, have increased from Rs. 6782 lakhs in 1992-93 to Rs. 9649 lakhs in 1996-97, an increase of 42% in five years which is indicative of the efforts put in by the Corporation to streamline the recoveries; with regard to repayment of borrowings, there was an increase of 7% in 1995-96 compared to the previous year, and a drop of 23% in 1996-97 compared to 1995-96. The deficit between recoveries and disbursements declined from 31% in 1994-95 to 7% in 1996-97, which is an encouraging sign.

Table 2.13
Recovery of Principal/Interest Vs Repayment of Borrowings

(Rs. in Lakhs)

S. No.	*Parameter*	*1992-93*	*1993-94*	*1994-95*	*1995-96*	*1996-97*
A.	Recoveries:					
(i)	of Principal	3283	2728	3751	4380	5352
(ii)	of Interest	3499	3137	4084	4478	4297
	Total	6782	5865	7835	8858	9649
B.	Payments:					
(i)	of Borrowings	3992	3866	3881	4184	791
(ii)	of Interest	2917	3292	3528	3713	2780
(iii)	Sub-Total	6909	7158	7409	7897	3571
(iv)	Disbursement of Loans	4708	4355	4012	6182	6781
	Total	11617	11513	11421	14079	10352
C.	Deficit (B-A)	4835	5648	3586	5221	703
D.	Deficit as % of Total Uses	42	49	31	37	7

Key Result Areas — Comparative Position

The overall efficiency of a non-banking financial institution (NBFI) can be evaluated by comparing it with a similar NBFI in respect of fourteen Key Result Areas. Key Result Areas of MPFC are compared with Andhra Pradesh State Financial Corporation (APSFC) and Uttar Pradesh Financial Corporation (UPFC) because MPFC and APSFC are of the same vintage, having started in 1955-56 and have more or less the same share capital, and both have been ranked in IDBI in B Category. UPFC has been taken for comparison because it is ranked in A Category and its performance is considered as that of one of the best SFCs in the country. In Annexure, fourteen Key Results Areas of MPFC are compared with APSFC and UPFC for two years, viz., 1995-96 and 1996-97 — it was static compared to the earlier year. In disbursements, MPFC has improved by 12% in 1996-97 compared to 1995-96. In interest recovery, there is a drop of 4% in 1996-97 compared to the earlier year. In the same period, recoveries towards principal have increased by 22%. In total income, MPFC has made a marginal improvement of 3% over the previous year. There has been a reduction in total expenditure by 20% in 1996-97 compared to the previous year. The drop is mainly noticed in interest on long-term loans. In personnel cost there is an increase of 36% in 1996-97 compared to 1995-96. In administration expenses, there is a drop of 1% in 1996-97. The number of applications sanctioned have dropped by 14% in 1996-97 over the previous year. The average loan amount per application sanctioned increased by 17%. Personnel cost per application is high Rs. 125507 in 1996-97 recording an increase of 58% over the previous year, whereas in APSFC the increase is of 13% while in UPFC unlike in MPFC and APSFC there is a reduction of 22% in personnel cost in 1996-97 compared to 1995-96 which clearly speaks of high employee productivity of UPFC.

Comments on Cash Flow Projections (1997-98 to 2004-05)

Cash flow projections, projected profitability and projected balance sheets for eight years (1997-98 to 2004-2005) may be seen at Annexures.., .. and .. It will be seen therefrom that projections are from 1997-98 to 2004-05 together with actuals of 1996-97.

Recovery, Bonds and Disbursements

MPFC's projections from 1997-98 to 2004-05, i.e. eight years, with base year of 1996-97 have been summarised in respect of three elements, i.e. Recovery, Bonds Issue, and

Disbursements which form a pertinent part of MPFC's performance.

Cash flow projections of recovery, Bonds Issue and Disbursements are recapitulated in Table 2.14.

Table 2.14
Cash Flow Projections of Recoveries, Bonds and Disbursements

Year	*Recoveries*		*Bonds*		*Disbursements*	
	Amount (Rs. in lakhs)	*Increase (%)*	*Amount (Rs. in lakhs)*	*Increase (%)*	*Amount (Rs. in lakhs)*	*Increase (%)*
1996-97	9630	-	1700	-6686	6686	-
1997-98	10061	04	-	-	9000	35
1998-99	12221	21	1035	-40	10350	15
1999-00	13941	14	3871	274	11385	10
2000-01	14272	02	4258	10	12524	10
2001-2	15823	11	4615	08	13776	10
2002-03	17748	12	6061	31	15153	10
2003-04	19677	11	8334	38	16669	10
2004-05	21630	10	8526	02	18336	10

3

Madhya Pradesh State Textile Corporation Limited

Prelude

The Madhya Pradesh State Textile Corporation Limited (MPSTC) was set up in 1970 under the Companies Act, 1956. The Corporation is under the administrative control of the Commerce and Industry Department of the Government of Madhya Pradesh. The Head Office (HO) of the company is located at Bhopal. It has an authorized share capital of Rs. 100 million. The initial paid-up capital of the company was Rs. 68.60 million, and it continues to be same till date.

Objectives

The following have been listed as the objectives of the company in the Memorandum of Association:

- To carry on the business of textile mills as entrusted to it either by the Central Government or by the State Government.
- To carry on the business of production of cloth from handloom and powerloom.
- To acquire, start or run schemes for the development of handloom and powerloom industry, and for the betterment of the condition of handloom and powerloom weavers in the State.

- To take over and run as an employment relief scheme or otherwise any textile mill in Madhya Pradesh State which is closed or likely to be closed or has gone into liquidation or otherwise.

- To manage and control any textile mill in Madhya Pradesh State which may be taken over by the Government under the Industries (Development and Regulation) Act, 1951.

- To raise finance for the above purpose through suitable means.

Discussion with the policy makers, company executives, textile experts and researchers and the study of the MOU documents of the company, indicate that in reality the major objectives have been:

- To manage, operate and rehabilitate the taken-over mills by the State Government.
- To efficiently run Avanti Spinning Mills and undertake its modernisation and expansion.
- To make available yarn to handloom and powerloom weavers.
- To provide assistance to the handloom weavers in the marketing of handloom cloth, and to train and provide employment opportunities to them.
- To assist the Central Government and the State Government in the implementation of handloom-related policies.
- To operate and expand the activities of the powerloom sector.

The main objectives pursued have been that of managing textile mills, handloom production units, showrooms and sales outlets.

Efforts do not appear to have been made to distinguish

between the primary and secondary objectives of the corporation, resulting in lack of prioritisation and diffusion in the focus of the company. Most of the objectives were developmental in nature or agency-related. They did not have commercial and financial orientation. In other words, whereas MPSTC emphasized the public purpose aspects, it was very weak on commercial enterprise considerations.

Profile of the Company

The company was set up as a State enterprise and has a wholly owned spinning mill known as Avanti Spinning Mill, Sanawad. It took over two private mills known as Shree Sajjan Mills Limited, Ratlam, and the Rajkumar Mills Limited, Indore. It had a nationalised mill in Ujjain named as Indore Textiles, which has since closed from 30.9.97. It has 24 showrooms within and outside the State and 20 handloom production units. It has 10 sub-units for production and procurement of handloom fabrics, spread all over the State. The major products of the company constitute handloom fabrics procured from various HPUs and yarn spun by the Avanti Spinning Mills and cotton cloth produced through the composite taken-over mills. The total annual turnover the company is Rs. 52 crore, of which Rs. 20 crore is contributed by the sale of handloom products and Rs. 20 crore from the overall yarn sales.

Management

The company is managed by a Board of Directors appointed by the Government of Madhya Pradesh. The number of members of the Board has remained constant at six between 1992-93 and 1996-97. Besides a Chairman, Vice-Chairman and Managing Director (nominated as officials), there are three members on the Board. Of the total six members, four are drawn from the Civil Service and the other two come from the political stream. Both the Chairman and Vice-Chairrman are politicians. The average tenure given to the Board members is two years. The handloom, powerloom and the silk sector industries are not represented on the Board.

There is no labour representation on the Board nor is there any public enterprise personnel representation. There are no functional Directors in the Company and hence the representation of the Directors on the Board does not arise. In terms of type, the company has a policy board as it does not have any functional directors.

There were frequent changes in the office of the Managing Director. In 1992-93, three persons occupied this position. In 1993-94 there was one change in this position, whereas in 1994-95 there was no replacement. In 1995-96 again there was one change, followed by no change in 1996-97. There is no comparison of the pay of the Managing Director with his counterpart in the private sector. Normally he is in the senior scale of the Indian Administrative Service Rs. 5900-6700 and his perquisites include subsidized housing and car.

Table 3.1 provides details about the total number of Directors appointed, total number of Board meetings held, and number of Directors who attended the Annual General Meeting, and important agenda items discussed during the various Board Meetings.

Table 3.1
Board of Directors

Particulars	*1992-93*	*1993-94*	*1994-95*	*1995-96*	*1996-97*
Total No. of Directors	4	4	4	3	2
Total No. of Meetings	5	4	2	2	4
No. of Directors that attended AGM	2	4	2	2	2
Important agendas' topic discussed	Handlooms Mills Accounts Personnel and Admn.	Handlooms Mills Accounts Personnel and Admn.	Handlooms Mills Accounts Personnel and Admn.	Handlooms Mills Accounts Personnel and Admn.	Handlooms Mills Accounts Personnel and Admn.

Table 3.1 reveals that all the six positions of the Board were never filled up. During 1995-96 and 1996-97 the number of memberships filled up on the Board were three and two respectively. The total number of Board Meeting held were the lowest in 1994-95 and 1995-96. No importance was attached to the Annual General Meeting which is evident from the fact that during most of the years and the number of Directors attending such meetings did not exceed the mark of two. The study of the agenda discussed points out that significant issues such as competitiveness, productivity, profitability, self-sustaining finances, organizational climate, work culture, corporate mission, value addition, technology upgradation, responsibility/accountability were never discussed at the Board level.

One important reason, among others, for the lack of a clear cut vision for the company is probably related to the peculiar phenomenon of a dual control on the company exercised by the Commissioner of Handlooms, Government of Madhya Pradesh and its Department of Commerce and Industry. This is further supported by the fact that the MOUs of the company are signed, on the one hand, on behalf of the enterprise by the Principal Secretary, Rural Industries Department, Government of Madhya Pradesh, and the Managing Director of MPSTC on the other.

An analysis of the organization chart points out that it does not provide for the marketing thrust of the enterprise which, in turn, has resulted in poor product development and design function, and inadequate commercial intelligence. Interaction with the company officials points out to the gross inadequacy of competent human resource for guiding manpower at the grassroot level in the departments of Marketing, Finance and Accounts, and Human Resource Development and Administration.

On March 31, 1997, the Corporation had 579 employees on its rolls, of which 69 (11.92%) were in the managerial cadre and 510 (88.08%) in the non-managerial cadre. The Avanti Spinning Mill had 78 (5.34%) managerial and 1382 (94.66%) non-managerial staff and labour on its rolls.

Table 3.2 gives the details of employment provided directly and indirectly:

Table 3.2
Direct and Indirect Employment

Year	*Total No. of Looms engaged*	*Employment provided*
1992-93	12,939	38,817
1993-94	11,694	35,082
1994-95	12,340	37,020
1995-96	11,207	33,621
1996-97	7,531	22,593

Government-Enterprise Interface

As noted earlier, the company has to interact with the Commissioner of Handlooms, Government of Madhya Pradesh and its Department of Commerce and Industry. It has to follow all the rules and regulations prescribed by the Finance Department, Government of Madhya Pradesh, with regard to incurring expenditure. The instructions issued by the General Administration Department have to be followed by the company with regard to the composition of the Board and directions given from time to time. Such instructions have been received in the past from the Chief Minister and the Minister. Though the pricing decisions are the prerogative of the Chief Executive of the Company, it has to follow the instructions issued by the Commissioner of Handlooms regarding production and sale of handloom fabrics and sale of yarn under the Mill Gate Price Scheme of the Government of India. Though hire of labour/officials is within the competence of the Board of Directors, the Company keeps on appointing deputationists as instructed by the Government from time to time. The company has to seek the permission of the Government for collaborations within the country and also for collaborations with foreign firms. The company has to interact constantly with the Commerce and Industry

Department for its administration and for seeking assistance to the sick textile mills. Currently, the Government-enterprise interface is being regulated through the MOU which specifies in Para 1 the objectives of the company, in Para 2 the targets for a particular financial year, in Para 3 expectations from the State Government and, finally, the complete matrix of the proposed targets and wages, etc.

Capital Structure and Finances

Table 3.3 portrays the capital structure of the Company:

Table 3.3
Capital Structure

Particulars	*1992-93*	*1993-94*	*1994-95*	*1995-96*	*1996-97*
Equity	685.95	685.95	685.95	685.95	685.95
Reserve & Surplus	68.27	68.27	67.37	67.42	67.42
Owner's equity	754.22	754.22	753.32	753.37	753.37
Total long-term loans	2466.51	2975.61	3458.03	4132.44	5734.06
Debt-Equity Ratio	3.24	3.94	4.59	5.54	7.48

Table 3.3 reveals that the company was highly levered in favour of debt. This did not turn out to be a good proposition for the company as its profit was negative all through the period 1992-93 to 1996-97 and the interest burden shadowed the gross profits in 1992-93 and 1993-94, and constituted a vast portion of gross profits during the remaining years of the study, i.e., 1994-95, 1995-96 and 1996-97. Normally gross profits should be three times of the interest in the case of health companies which was a far cry in the case of MPSTC.

The composition of the long-term debt and equity points out that the company did not tap sources of equity such as the Central Government, financial institutions, general investing public, foreign collaborators, etc., and all its equity came from the State Government, which remained constant from its inception till date. The value addition in terms of earnings has remained disappointing which could be seen from the fact that the reserves and surplus total to a mere 10% of the equity of the company over a time span of 27 years. A study of the funds capitalized through long-term debt points out that the company's dependence again has been limited to the State Government and it has drawn a blank from other sources. The company has ignored the canons of the debt-equity restructuring which is seen from the fact that the debt-equity ratio of 3.24 in 1992-93 touched a mark of 7.48 in 1996-97.

Profitability and Total Financial Performance

The gross margin, gross profits, and the profits after tax have all remained negative for the company as a whole during the period 1992-93 to 1996-97. As a result, the net worth of the company declined to become chronically negative during the period 1992-93 to 1996-97. Table 3.4 shows the data on the profitability and the total financial performance of the company.

Table 3.4
Profitability and Financial Performance

(Rs. in Lakhs)

Particulars	*1992-93*	*1993-94*	*1994-95*	*1995-96*	*1996-97*
Gross margin	-53.20	-76.83	-619.23	-467.12	-492.56
Gross profit	-178.36	-229.93	-378.75	-613.93	-663.91
Profit after tax	-431.18	-510.83	-720.26	-1053.73	-1170.43
Net worth	-530.06	-1040.89	-937.64	-1991.32	-3161.75

The net worth has been eroded to such an extent that the company has joined the group of cases referred to the Board for Industrial and Financial Reconstruction (BIFR).

Both the margin and turnover was continually unfavourable, leading to negative net worth. The cost of goods sold turned out to be higher than sales during the entire period of 1992-93 to 1996-97. The company loosely controlled its raw material consumption and over-spent on salaries, wages and allowances, and also incurred administrative expenses on the higher side. Its working capital turnover declined from approximately 2.80 times in 1992-93 to 1.30 times in 1996-97. One of the reasons of tardy working capital management was a huge investment in loans and advances which increased from Rs. 3200.90 lakhs in 1992-93 to Rs. 3769.26 lakhs in 1996-97.

The percentage of debts for five years to total debts for Indore Textiles were 60.86%, for the handloom sector 57.14%, and for Shree Sajjan Mills 72.19%.

Table 3.5 reveals that both the handloom and mill sectors were incurring cash losses with little hope for the company earning positive gross margin, gross profits and net profits.

Table 3.5
Cash Losses

(Rs. in Lakhs)

Year	*Handloom Sector*	*Mill Sector*	*Total*
1992-93	+7.03	438.21	431.18
1993-94	110.82	400.01	510.83
1994-95	98.05	622.21	720.26
1995-96	204.53	849.20	1053.73
1996-97	283.92	886.51	1170.43

Interaction with functionaries of the company pointed out that excessive cost of direct inputs and low productivity of the plant and machinery was responsible for cash losses in the mill sector. Excessive overheads and obsolete machinery and absence of demand for the various products were responsible for cash losses in the handloom sector.

Present Activities and Performance

Mill Sector

The company owns two mills, viz., Avanti Spinning Mills and Indore Textiles. It manages two taken-over mills, viz., Rajkumar Mills and Shree Sajjan Mills.

Avanti Spinning Mills

This mill was established in 1964 and is a wholly owned enterprise of MPSTC. It has 25,000 spindles, with a spinning capacity to manufacture 25s average carded counts. The company has an accumulated profit of Rs. 70 million and has been a professionally managed concern. However, in the recent past the performance of the unit has suffered a setback due to forced diversion of this mill's funds to the handloom sector. To put the enterprise back on a firm footing, an injection of Rs. 24 million is required towards working capital. The enterprise also needs to carry out modernisation, with a capital expenditure of Rs. 64 million. According to the management of MPSTC, the mill could go in for expansion to the extent of 12,500 spindles.

Indore Textiles

This mill was set up in 1924 as a gray cloth manufacturing unit with 25,000 spindles and 500 plain looms. This mill was nationalized and merged with the company in 1986. Since its merger the mill has continued to remain a sick unit and has been a perpetual burden on the State Government which reimbursed cash losses incurred by the company till its closure with effect from September 30, 1997. During the 11 years of its operation it incurred losses of about Rs. 520 million. It decided to pay off 1300 workmen dues worth Rs. 135 million at the time of closure. It is expected that the sale of fixed assets i.e. land, building and scrap machinery may leave the Government with a sum of Rs. 120 million after clearing off the dues.

Rajkumar Mills Limited

This is a taken-over mill entrusted to the company to manage its operations. The owners of the company pledged their shares with the State Government with voting rights to enable the State Government to nominate its Board of Directors. This company was set up in 1926 under private management with 25,000 spindles, 628 plain looms and process house to process about 40,000 metres of cloth per day, engaging 1580 workmen per day. The mill has accumulated losses of Rs. 410 million and is incurring Rs. 2.5 million a month as cash losses which are being partially reimbursed by the State Government. The main reasons for incurring losses include too old machinery and obsolete technology, non-implementation of modernisation plans, and paucity of funds to run the mill at its full capacity. The cash losses reimbursed by the State Government have amounted to Rs. 167 million. The Government approached BIFR for the revival of the company, which sanctioned a rehabilitation package of Rs. 262 million to instal 24 high-speed air-jet looms and to do away with its processing capacity, as a result of which the complement of workmen has to come down from 1580 to 824. The means of finance proposed to fund the package comprise Rs. 170 million by way of sale of surplus land, Rs. 27 million by way of sale of old machinery and scrap, and Rs. 65.5 million through interest-free loans from the State Government. Further, it is expected that the State Government would approve the proposal of conversion of loans and equity, deferment of sales tax liability and permission to sell surplus land.

Shree Sajjan Mills

The company is a taken-over mill from private management set up in 1928 with 30,000 spindles, 478 looms and processing machinery to process about 50,000 metres of cloth per day, engaging 1622 workmen per day. Since its take-over in 1989 to save jobs of the workmen employed, it has accumulated losses of over Rs. 580 million. The cash losses reimbursed by the State Government have been to the tune of Rs. 260 million. It has been incurring cash losses at the rate of Rs. 3 million per month which are being partially reimbursed by the State Government. The reasons for incurring losses are the same as those in the case of the

Rajkumar Mills. On being referred to BIFR, winding up was suggested for this unit. However, on the direction of the State Government, the management of the mill went into appeal before AAIFR who finally approved the rehabilitation package worth Rs. 270 million which proposes to convert this composite textile mill into a modern unit and to reduce the daily workers' engagement from 1580 to 680. The proposed means of finance to fund the package include Rs. 150 million from sale of surplus land, Rs. 22 million by way of sale of old machinery and scrap, Rs. 51.20 million from interest-free loan from the State Government and Rs. 48.60 million through internal resources generated by the mill. The mill has sought various concessions and equity participation from the State Government and also its permission from the sale of surplus land.

Handloom Sector

The company has 32 handloom production units (HPUs) spread over the entire State of Madhya Pradesh which provide training and skill upgradation to the handloom weavers, yarn and other raw material and buy back the finished clothing and marketing assistance by way of sale of handloom products to retain outlets, and thrust in the implementation of the policies of the State Government with regard to the handloom sector.

The handloom production programme of this sector comprises two main groups, viz., Janata Cloth Production and Non-Janata Cloth Production. The Janata Cloth Production scheme was started by the Government in the early 1970s under which the company touched the peak manufacture of about 18 million sq. mtrs of cloth. However, this scheme is being phased out to touch zero production level during the year 1997-98. Table 3.6 gives details of the Janata Cloth production during the period 1992-93 to 1996-97.

Non-Janata cloth production includes manufacture of some major textile items for sale in the open market such as sarees, dress material, bedsheets and furnishings. The raw

Table 3.6
Janata Cloth Production

(Rs. in lakhs)

Year	No. of looms engaged	Annual production capacity in lakh sq. mtrs.	Annual production in lakh sq. mtrs.	Average production per loom/annum
1992-93	8365	250.95	152.77	1826
1993-94	8057	241.71	144.27	1790
1994-95	6600	198.00	87.90	1332
1995-96	6233	186.99	57.37	920
1996-97	4794	143.82	38.38	772

material and designs are provided to the handloom weavers and in return MPSTC purchases saleable items directly from them. The production/procurement of non-Janata textile items has increased form 30 million sq. mtrs. to 100 million sq. mtrs. but is insufficient to meet the establishment and marketing costs. The production of non-Janata cloth items has not risen commensurately due to competition from rivals and liquidity crunch, as a result of which the production drastically declined to 45 million sq. mtrs. in 1996-97 as compared to 61.6 million sq. mtrs. in the year 1992-93. Annexure I gives details of the HPUs and their expected production in 1997-98.

Marketing

Marketing takes place only in the case of Avanti Spinning Mills. The marketing of handloom products is done through various showrooms/sales counters widely spread out in major cities of the State and the country. Details of show-rooms and their expected turnover for the year 1997-98 as is given in Annexure-2. An intensive review of the performance of the company is given in Annexure-3. The interaction with the company management and policy makers clearly points out that the performance of the enterprise on the whole has remained very poor in terms of both the fiscal and financial parameters. The company also suffered from dearth of funds and could never be financially viable. Its dependence on the Government increased year after year which could be seen from the fact that not only the entire equity and the debt funds came from the State, but also revenue subsidies on Janata cloth were extended by the Government to the company. The extent of revenue subsidy on Janata cloth aggregated to around Rs. 1665 lakhs for the period 1992-93 to 1996-97. It is always advisable to give direct subsidies to the weavers/spinners. The capacity utilized by the mill sector of the company, both owned and managed mills, has been declining. The output of the handloom sector production units is fast declining and the marketing efforts are not commensurate to meet the shortfall registered in the mill and handloom sectors. The per capita turnover of the employees was declining. Though one of the social objectives of the company is to provide employment, the number of weavers and spinners engaged in the activities of the company constituted a very small fraction of the total number of weavers and spinners in the State. The contention that the company has not an encouraging presence among weavers is supported by the fact that the average earnings of weavers in the company is very low as compared to weavers working in HPUs in the private sector or counterparts of the mill workers in the private sector.

Proposals for Restructuring and Rehabilitation

The discussions with the company management and the policy makers revealed that efforts have been initiated to rehabilitate the various units of MPSTC. In order to do this, a fresh look was initiated to formulate objectives relevant to the present-day setting. The reformulated objectives are started below:

- To upgrade the Avanti Spinning Mill to manufacture coarse to superfine quality yarn and to provide yarn at reasonable price directly to the handloom weavers or Society of Handloom Weavers and to export or sell the balance quantity of the yarn produced.

- To purchase on cash down payment terms at most reasonable price handloom products from the producers.
- To entrust the HO of MPSTC with the task of market intelligence and design, handloom purchases and to make available required raw material at reasonable prices to the handloom weavers.

In order to discharge these obligations, MPSTC would have to set up two subsidiaries, viz., Avanti Spinning Mills and Avanti Handlooms Company.

The main purpose of the rehabilitation exercise is:

- To get rid to sick textile mills existing in the present portfolio of MPSTC.
- To do away with the concept of HPUs.
- To prune the HO and field staff by paying voluntary retirement benefits, and to create a new work culture amongst the leftover staff.
- To rehabilitate Rajkumar Mills and Shree Sajjan Mills to be finally sold to willing entrepreneurs or to be closed down.

Rehabilitation of Rajkumar Mills

The highlights of the rehabilitation proposal are indicated below:

Proposals

Particulars	*Present Capacity*	*Proposed capacity after rehabilitation*
Spinning (spindles)	25,000	15,360
Weaving capacity (looms)	628 plain looms	24 Nos. wide width air-jet looms.
Processing capacity (mtrs. per day)	40,000	Nil
Manpower complement (daily engagement)	1,582	824

Project Cost Estimates

S. No.		*Expenditure Head*	*Amount (Rs. in million)*
a.	(i)	Development of land	0.90
	(ii)	Building repair	18.90
	(iii)	Plant and Machinery	130.60
	(iv)	Miscellaneous fixed assets	4.00
	(v)	Contingencies	17.00
		Total	171.40
b.	(i)	Payment of PF/ESI dues	7.80
	(ii)	Retrenchment of surplus workers	22.50
		Total	30.30
c.	(i)	Cash losses during rehabilitation	31.80
	(ii)	Margin money against working capital	28.40
		Total	60.20
		Grand Total (a+b+c)	262.00

Means of Finance

Means	*Amount (Rs. in million)*
By sale of surplus land	169.60
By sale of old machinery	26.90
Interest free loan from State Government	65.50
Mill's own contribution	-
Total	262.00

There are the following three options of permanent closure of this mill:

Options

Option	*Closing method*	*Financial implications (Rs. in million)*
1.	Under Section 25(O) of the Industrial Disputes Act	192.007
2.	To obtain winding up orders from BIFR	103.357
3.	To hand over all the shares to the original promoters	71.619

Rehabilitation of Shree Sajjan Mills

The highlights of the rehabilitation proposal pertaining to Shree Sajjan Mills are indicated below:

Proposals

Particulars	*Present capacity*	*Proposed capacity after rehabilitation*
Spinning (spindles)	25,000	25,000
Weaving capacity (looms)	478 plain looms	Nil
Processing capacity (mtrs. per day)	50,000	Nil
Manpower complement (daily engagement)	1,622	680

Project Cost Estimates

S. No.	*Expenditure Head*	*Amount (Rs. in million)*
1	2	3
a. (i)	Replacement of spinning machinery	80.00
(ii)	Replacement of engineering equipment	3.35
(iii)	Provision for contingencies	16.65
(iv)	Renovation of Spinning Department	19.10
(v)	Renovation of building, etc.	6.35
	Total	125.45

1	2	3
b. (i)	Repayment of old loans with interest to SBI	94.08
(ii)	Down payment of PF/ESI dues	8.76
(iii)	Labour rationalisation	32.32
(iv)	Margin money for working capital	3.35
(v)	Contingency expenses	5.84
	Total	144.35
	Grand Total (a+b)	269.80

Means of Finance

Means	*Amount (Rs. in million)*
By sale of surplus land	150.00
By sale of old machinery	22.00
Interest free loan from State Government	51.20
Old FD	24.20
Internal accruals	22.40
Total	269.80

There are the following three options of permanent closure of this mill:

Options

Option	*Closing method*	*Financial implications (Rs. in million)*
1	Under Section 25(O) of the Industrial Disputes Act	286.150
2	To obtain winding up orders from BIFR	179.000
3	To hand over all the share to the original promotes	165.837

Avanti Spinning Mills

The Avanti Spinning Mills could be hived off from MPSTC to be sold to a well-established private sector counterpart through a public bid on outright sale or be handed over to such a company on management contract or lease. The option of inviting the management contract or lease. The option of inviting the managers/workers to form a cooperative society to run the mill should also be examined as was done in the case of the Bhaskar Textile Mills, Orissa, formerly a Government of Orissa enterprise.

Rehabilitation of MPSTC

The yearly expenses of MPSTC, HO, HPUs and Showrooms are as under:

(Rs. in Lakhs)

Expenses Head	*HO*	*Central Stores*	*HPU*	*Showrooms*
Staff wages	102.00	13.10	165.60	110.40
Fringe benefits	10.00	2.50	6.00	5.00
Admn. Expenses like TA, DA, phone, insurance, house rent, etc.	60.00	12.00	24.00	16.00
Interest	45.00	-	-	-
House Rent	6.00	1.80	6.00	30.00
Cloth processing & printing expenses	-	60.00	-	30.00
Sales discount	-	-	-	150.00
Total	223.00	89.40	201.60	341.40
Grand Total		Rs. 88.54 million		

Break-even Point

Particulars	*Amount (Rs. in million)*
Total expenses	88.54
Minimum expected profit to reach break-even point	88.54
Average profit mark-up at Showrooms	50%
Minimum expected sales	$\frac{88.54 \times 150}{50}$
i.e.	265.50
Add: 10% margin for wastage	26.55
Total expected sales	292.05

With limited available resources, it is impossible to achieve this figure and as such the company is left with no alternative but to bring down its expenses drastically. A heavy reduction in staff/manpower has been suggested as shown below:

Reduction in Staff/Manpower

Designation	*Existing No.*	*Proposed*	*Reduction*
1	2	3	4
Chairman	1	Nil	1
Vice-Chairman	1	Nil	1
Personal Staff of Chairman & Vice-Chairman	16(8)*	Nil	16
Managing Director	1	1	Nil
Managing Director's staff	10	7	3
General Manager (Mills/Mkt)	1	1	Nil
General Manager's (Mills/Mkt) Staff including Deputy Managers to Peons	10	6	4
General Manager (Per. & Admn.)	1	Nil	1

Contd...

1	2	3	4
Manager (Per. & Admn.)	1	1	Nil
Pers. & Admn. Staff including Deputy Managers to Peons	28	15	13
Company Secretary	1	1	Nil
Secretarial Staff	2	1	1
Controller of Accounts & Finance (Accounts)	1	1	Nil
Controller of Accounts & Finance (Audit)	1	Nil	1
Accounts Staff in Accounts & Audit from Deputy Manager to Peons	35	20	15
General Manager (Handlooms)	1	Nil	1
Manager (Production)	1	Nil	1
Handlooms Production Staff	19(1)*	Nil	19
Manager-Marketing	1	1	Nil
Marketing Staff at HO	19	13	6
Field Staff at HPUs	246(11)*	Nil	246
Field Staff at Showrooms	189(32)*	157	32
Proposed Staff at HO and Major Handloom Centres for procurement of product from weavers	Nil	24*	Nil
Total	586	249	361
*Contingency Staff			-24

			337

Retrenchment of a Total of 337 Officers/Staff is Required

As a part of the rehabilitation process of the company, the Government can withdraw Chairman, Vice-Chairman and two senior officers from the Commerce and Industry Department on deputation. 46 contingent staff need not be retained. As such, a total of 326 staff members can be voluntarily retired by paying a sum of about Rs. 90 million.

Should MPSTC be Retained?

In the previous section the two options of retaining the various units/activities or their closure based on the suggestions emanating from the management of the company and the policymakers have been examined. There is a need to make a clear-cut choice. To remain objective it is necessary that a logical framework is evolved and applied to the company to arrive at a fair decision. Normally three questions should be asked in order to decide about the continuation or closure of a company:

- Has the company mobilised resources other than from the State or Central Government?
- Has the company earned profits?
- Does the company serve the public purpose?

Some benchmarks could be laid down to test the position of MPSTC on these three parameters. A 20% mobilisation of resources from other than the Government could be taken as satisfactory for the company's continuation in regard to the measure of resource mobilisation. A 10% earning of profit before interest and taxes could justify the company's continuation with regard to the profit test. Insofar as public purpose is concerned, it would be relevant to ensure as to whether the company fulfils the objectives of the present National Textile Policy and serves the cause of the people in general and the sections of society connected to it, i.e. handloom weavers and spinners in particular.

The company does not justify its continuation on the resource mobilisation front as its resources is entirely come from the State Government. Its profit-earning has been very poor and during the period 1992-93 to 1996-97 it has incurred losses all through. The New Textile Policy, for the first time in the post-independence period, emphasizes profitability in sharp contrast to the hitherto thrust on employment. Both its handloom and mills sectors were not delivering the goods at the most economic price and in the most efficient manner.

Thus, viewed from the angle of public policy the company does not justify its continuation.

One of the reason being put forth for the continuation of MPSTC is to ensure an economic price being given to the handloom weavers who are not forced to do distress sales. This argument is not admissible because the non-cooperatised handloom sector is a smaller segment of the total handloom sector in Madhya Pradesh. Further, there is a multiplicity of organizations engaged in selling the handloom products in the State. For instance, the Laghu Udyog Nigam and the Hastaship Vikas Nigam have their own outlets similar to those set up by MPSTC, competing not only within the State but also outside the State, and that too under the same name, i.e. "Mrignayani". The Khadi and Village Industries Commission, the Khadi and Village Industries Board and the Apex Federation of Handloom Weavers are also competing in the field of procurement and sale of handloom products.

With the Janata cloth production scheme, which formed the backbone of the handloom sector, having already been phased out, a big question arises about the sustainability of the present product line of the Corporation. In terms of market structure, the company is in the competitive sector. The presence of private sector, both national and in Madhya Pradesh, in the field of textiles of all types is so strong, that it would be difficult to take on such competition. Its continuation would only result in a perpetual subsidisation by the State Government which is not economically viable or feasible or politically advisable.

The company fails to qualify on all the three tests and, therefore, it is evident that there is no justification for the company to continue in its present shape and it is a fit case for closure. This leads us to the question as to how such closure could be attempted. There cannot be one uniform approach to do this.

In our view, the work undertaken by HPUs is developmental in nature and has a very small commercial angle, and could be handed over to the Rural Industries Department of the Government which could be the most appropriate agency. It could train the weavers and spinners in the State, start courses for their education, procure raw materials for distribution to them, arrange to purchase raw materials for distribution to them, arrange to purchase finished goods from such weavers and spinners, and then market them or provide marketing assistance to them. No body would disagree that the upliftment of weavers and spinners is a very important task but certainly this could be done better by the Government as it requires huge resources and extension of subsidies.

There is no reason for MPSTC to run the taken-over textile mills. These could be better handed over to their erstwhile owners or closed down. The sale of land and machinery itself could fund the closure to a large extent. With the upgradation of textile technology, existence of very strong competitors in the private sector and the lack of the requisite work culture, there is no reason to retain them in the public enterprise portfolio of the State Government. The experience gained from the closure of Indore Textiles could be used in closure of the two taken-over mills, viz., Rajkumar Mills and Shree Sajjan Mills.

Coming to the HO/Corporate Office, it is suggested that the Government can offer VRS to the 337 officials/staff identified. The remaining 249 executives/staff members could be absorbed by the Government in the Rural Industries Department, Khadi and Village Industries Board and the Commerce and Industry Department.

We may further note in this connection that the government of India is in the process of making up its mind to withdraw itself from the running of the National Textile Corporation Limited which has under its umbrella about 108 taken-over mills. It has already offered VRS to a large chunk of employees working in these mills, funded by the National Renewal Fund. The Government of Madhya Pradesh will do well to think on these lines as the thrust of the present Textile

Policy of the Government is not on providing employment, but on improving productivity and competitiveness of the textile sector.

The company does not have to look far for experience in this regard as back home the experience of the closure and offer of VRS to the employees of Indore Textiles with effect from September 30, 1997 would come in very handy.

The Gujarat State Textile Corporation offered VRS in two stages. In the first stage, it offered severance to 4500 employees. This was followed by a restructuring exercise of closing down such mills and sections which were continuously incurring losses. However, this did not bring about the required change. Consequently, in the second stage, the corporation offered VRS to a huge number of employees, i.e. around 5000. It is aid that the corporation carried out the VRS with the consent of its employees. It was because of the realization of both the Corporation and Government on the one hand, and the employees on the other, that it was difficult to run a State Textile in a highly competitive environment which required quick reflexes on the part of the management, controlled and guided by the Government to understand the market impulses and accordingly take decisions.

It is also relevant to refer to the proposed move suggested by the committee for Restructuring State Level Public Enterprises of the Government of Andhra Pradesh regarding the Andhra Pradesh Textile Development Corporation. There is a move to wind up the Corporation by selling the existing assets and the amount so realized is proposed to be utilized for offering severance compensation to the employees. The Government of Andhra Pradesh has been considering the suggestion of handing over the Janata scheme activity of the corporation to the State Handloom Department or the Andhra Pradesh Weavers' Cooperative Society. The Government proposes to immediately initiate action for disposal of the assets of the corporation and reduce further losses by implementing the lay-off/retrenchment scheme and also stoppage of commercial activities. It is also proposes to initiate action under Chapter III of Section 484 of the Companies Act, 1956, for virtual liquidation.

The non-performance of the textile mills in the other states has been the main reason for closing down the State Textile Corporation in their present form. Annexure-4 shows that the State Textile Mills owned by Gujarat, Haryana, Jammu & Kashmir, Karnataka, Kerala, Orissa, and West Bengal were a losing proposition. Annexure-5 briefly outlines the performance of the Textile Corporations in various other States.

Conclusion and Recommendations

MPSTC was set up in 1970 with the main objectives of managing textile mills, handloom production units, and showroom and sales outlets. A critical study of the objectives of the company points out that most of them were developmental in nature or agency-related. The element of commercial and financial viability was lacking.

MPSTC has two owned mills, namely, Avanti Spinning Mills and Indore Textiles, and it manages two taken-over mills, namely, Rajkumar Mills and Shree Sajjan Mills. It has 32 HPUs spread over the entire State of Madhya Pradesh.

The company is managed by a Board of Directors appointed by the Government of Madhya Pradesh. Its membership of six persons drawn from the civil service and politicians does not provide room for textile experts, spinners, weavers, consumers, and workers. The average tenure given to the Board members was two years. There have been frequent changes in the case of the Managing Director whose perquisites and pay are not competitive with his counterparts in the private sector. The Board of Directors has not been meeting regularly. The number of meetings also was either below the required mark or just the minimum necessary during the various years of the study. The number of Directors attending the meeting was the bare minimum. The Study of the agenda discussed points out that significant issues such as competitiveness, productivity, profitability, self-sustaining finances, organizational climate, work culture, corporate mission, value addition, technology upgradation, responsibility/accountability and future thrust were never discussed by the members of the Board. The company faced the peculiar phenomena of dual control exercised by the Commissioner of Handlooms and the Department of Commerce and Industry. The organizational structure of the company does not provide for functional Directors and production development and Corporate Plan.

MPSTC suffers from a weak Government-enterprise interface mechanism and process. It is over administered and under-managed. The complete dependence of the company on the Government for strategic issues such as mobilization of finances, appointments on the Board, staffing of the organization and organization of its portfolio of activities has deprived it from becoming an organic entity. The attempts to improve this interface through the MOU have not yielded the expected results on account of the lack of adequate commitment and involvement of both the Government and MPSTC.

The capital structure is highly levered in favour of debt and is not enterprise-friendly. The high debt-equity ratio resulted in huge interest burden undermining the profitability of the company to a significant extent. The company wholly depended on the State Government for the mobilization of financial resources and did not tap the Central Government, financial institutions, general investing public, etc., for funding purposes. The company's equity has remained constant during the five year period of the study, and the value addition in terms of earnings is reflected by reserves and surplus constituting some 10% of the equity, points to a minimum value addition.

The gross margin, gross profits, and profits after tax all remained negative for the company during the period 1992-93 to 1996-97. Consequently, the net worth of the company declined. The company had a chronically negative net worth during the entire period of the study. The net worth of the company has been eroded to such an extent that the Government of Madhya Pradesh has referred it to BIFR.

The chief factors for chronic loss-making in the company related to both the margin and turnover which continued to be unfavourable to the company during the entire period of the study. The cost of goods sold turned out to be higher than sales during the entire period from 1992-93 to 1996-97 as the company loosely controlled its raw material consumption and overspent on salaries, wages and allowances, and also incurred administrative expenses on the higher side. Its working capital management was shoddy as evidenced by the working capital turnover coinciding with the presence of huge investment in loans and large amounts overdue for more than five years.

There is no hope of the financial revival of the company as both its handloom and mill sectors incurred cash losses during the period 1993-94 to 1996-97. Excessive overheads and obsolete machinery, and also absence of demand for the various products led to the incurrence of cash losses.

The Avanti Spinning Mills is a wholly owned enterprise of MPSTC. Until recently it was a profit-making enterprise. However, in the recent past the performance of the unit suffered a setback. Indore Textiles was closed with effect from September 30, 1997.

Its marketing responsibilities include the management of the outlets of the Avanti Spinning Mills, and the marketing of handloom products through various showrooms and sales counters. Under the Mill Sector, Indore, Textiles was closed down in September 1997. The Rajkumar Mills, a taken-over mill, incurred losses all through due to old machinery and obsolete technology, non-implementation of modernization plans, and paucity of funds. It could continue to breathe due to the cash losses reimbursed to MPSTC by the State Government. The company was referred to BIFR, which sanctioned a rehabilitation package. Shree Sajjan Mills is a takenover unit incurring cash losses throughout the period of the study. It has been incurring cash losses at the rate of Rs. 3 million per month, which are being partially reimbursed by the State Government. BIFR suggested winding up, against which an appeal was made to AAIFR which finally provided a rehabilitation package.

The handloom production programme of the handloom sector comprises two main groups, Janata Cloth Production and Non-Janata Cloth Production. The Janata Cloth Production is being phased out to touch zero production level during the year 1997-98. The production of Non-Janata Cloth items has not risen commensurately due to fierce competition from rivals and liquidity crunch which resulted in a drastic reduction in the production under this scheme.

The discussion with the company management and the policy makers revealed that efforts have been initiated to rehabilitate the various units of MPSTC. The rehabilitation of Rajkumar Mills requires Rs. 262 million. The permanent closure of this mill under Section 25(O) of the ID Act is expected to cost Rs. 192 million. Its closure under winding up orders from BIFR is expected to cost Rs. 103 million. The cost of handing over all the shares to the original promoters will cost around Rs. 72 million. The rehabilitation of Shree Sajjan Mills requires Rs. 270 million. The closure of the mill under winding up order from BIFR is expected to cost Rs. 179 million. The cost of handing over all the shares to the original promoters will cost about Rs. 166 million.

The Avanti Spinning Mill could be hived off from MPSTC to be sold to a well-established private sector countrpart through a public bid on outright sale or be handed over to such a company on management contract or lease. The option of forming a cooperative society of workers/managers also merits consideration, as has been done in the case of Bhaskar Textile Mills, Orissa, formerly a Government of Orissa enterprise.

The continuation of the activities of MPSTC (HO, HPUs and Showrooms) of MPSTC rquire earning of a minimum profit of around Rs. 88 million, which would require the materialisation of total expected sales of Rs. 292 million. It is impossible to achieve this figure under the present constraints, unless a heavy reduction is achieved in the expenses incurred and VRS given to 337 employees.

The application of the three-dimension matrix, namely, the mobilization of resources from source other than the State Government, earning profits and serving public purpose, points out that MPSTC is a fit case for divestiture. The company incurred losses all through the five year span of the study and is in very poor shape, which is reinforced by the fact of the cash losses incurred in all the departments of its activities between 1992-93 and 1996-97. The net worth recorded a severe depletion. The company did not mobilize resources from any source other than the State Government. The company failed to serve much public purpose as the non-cooperatised handloom sector was comparataively smaller, income generation of the weavers and spinners depending on the company did not record any appreciable incurease, and turned out to be far lower than their counterparts in the unorganized private sector. Further, there was no reason to disburse subsidies to the corporation to make up the cash losses as such subsidies could be disbursed directly to the weavers and producers. There were superior scheme available to the Government to fulfil the developmental tasks entrusted to the corporation as the Khadi and Village Industries Commission, Khadi and Village Industries Board, Apex Federation of Handloom Weavers, and the Handloom Department, were already functioning in the State. Further, the multiplicity of marketing organization, suggests that an immediate closure of marketing activities was required under the umbrella of MPSTC.

A mix of divestiture methods would have to be applied to the case of MPSTC. The HPUs could be handled over to the Rural Industries Department/Khadi and Village Industries Commission/Khadi and Village Industries Board/Apex Federation of Handloom Weavers, as the work undertaken by these units is purely developmental in nature and has a very small commercial angle involved in it. There is no reason for the company to run these taken-over mills. They could be better handed over to their erstwhile owners or closed down. The sale of land and machinery itself could fund their closure. The Avanti Spinning Mills could be dealt with as suggested at 17.13.

The company does not have far to look for experience in this connection, as back home the experience of the closure and offer of VRS to the employees of Indore Textiles with effect from September 30, 1997 would come in very handy in this regard.

The Gujarat State Textile Corporation offered VRS in two states. In the first stage, it offered severance to 4500 employees. This was followed by a restructuring exercise of closing down such mills and sections which were continually incurring losses. However, this did not bring about the required change. Consequently, in the second stage, the company offered VRS to a huge number of employees, i.e. around 5000.

Annexure-1

Details of HPUs and their expected production in 1997-98

S. No.	*Name of Unit*	*Name of Sub-unit*	*Expected Production (Rs. in Lakhs)*
1.	Rajgarh	Champa	250.00
		Chandrapur	
2.	Bilaspur	Ambikapur	5.00
3.	Rajpur	Deobogh	20.00
		Bhilaigarh	
4.	Jagdalpur		Nil
5.	Durg		10.00
6.	Rajnandgaon		5.00
7.	Waraseoni		10.00
8.	Sidhi		5.00
9.	Chhindwara		Nil
10.	Sausar		2.00
11.	Lodhikheda		2.00
12.	Sidhi		10.00
13.	Sehore		Nil
14.	Ujjain	Indore	50.00
15.	Mandsaur		5.00
16.	Maheshwar		40.00
17.	Sarangpur	Shajapur	20.00
18.	Gwalior		10.00
19.	Chanderi		50.00
20.	Dhar	Jhabua	Nil
Total	20	10	474.00

Note: Six HPUs account for production of Rs. 430 lakhs or 90% of the total production.

Annexure-2

Details of Showrooms and expected turnover for 1997-98

S.No.	*Name of the Showroom*	*Expected Turnover (Rs. in lakhs)*
1.	Avanti, Bhopal	150.00
2.	Avanti, Indore	163.00
3.	Avanti, Bhilai	70.00
4.	Avanti, Gwalior	60.00
5.	Avanti, Ujjain	30.00
6.	Sales Counter, Maheshwar	20.00
7.	Avanti, Jabalpur	25.00
8.	Avanti, Raipur	63.00
9.	Avanti, Sagar	40.00
10.	Avanti, Rajgarh	42.00
11.	Avanti, Sehore	25.00
12.	Sales Counter, Shajapaur	15.00
13.	Avanti, Satna	15.00
14.	Sales Counter, Seoni	15.00
15.	Sales Counter, Waraseoni	10.00
16.	Avanti, Jagdalpur	15.00
17.	Sales Counter, Mandsour	10.00
18.	Sales Counter, Chanderi	10.00
19.	Sales Counter, Bilaspur	10.00
20.	Avanti, New Delhi (Lajpat Nagar)	100.00
21.	Avanti, New Delhi (Kanishka)	53.00
22.	Avanti, Jaipur	100.00
23.	Avanti, Bangalore	60.00
24.	Avanti, Calcutta	50.00
25.	Avanti, Jodhpur	30.00
26.	Avanti, Hyderabad	60.00
27.	Avanti, Cochin	30.00
28.	Avanti, Jodhpur	20.00
29.	Avanti, Trivandrum	20.00
30.	Avanti, Nagpur	36.00
31.	Avanti, Mumbai	50.00
32.	Avanti, Kanpur	30.00
33.	Avanti, Udaipur	40.00
34.	NH Expo	100.00
35.	HO	400.00
36.	Central Stores, Bhopal	Nil
37.	Others	Nil
	Total	1967.00

Annexure-3

Madhya Pradesh State Textile Corporation Limited Scheme-wise Profit & Loss Statement for the Year 1996-97

Details	*HPU*	*Showroom*	*HO*	*Total*	*IT Ujjain*	*ASM Sanawad*	*AP Ujjain*	*Grand Total*
Opening stock	80896708	39722909	-	120619617	2873294	9439009	-	132931920
Consumption	-	-	-	-	11312022	158234059	-	169546081
Purchases	119515306	14746943	30240663	16450291	-	-	-	164502911
Production & Procurement	5905812	2829009	122546	8857367	27852198	23191798	-	59901363
Repairs & Maintenance	339823	59172	271483	670478	53166	2791478	5015	3520137
Employees' Remuneration & benefits	16112739	7782996	13606740	37502475	18586181	11479371	68670	67636697
Admn. expenses	4397478	4373848	3660549	12431875	125523	1914172	24208	15625478
Selling & distribution	6835903	19477294	2191938	28505135	118794	885256	-	29509185
Financial expenses	45405	50324	6486374	6582103	40229823	3730892	-	50542818
Auditors	18000	20500	70500	109000	-	8000	-	117000
Sales Tax & Entry tax	-	-	163669	163669	-	-	-	163669
Depreciation	75659	206099	346264	628022	114703	947064	-	1689789
IUT purchases	-	54407764	4460532	58868296	-	-	-	58868296
Total	234142831	143679858	61577382	439400071	102395404	212621099	97893	754555344

Annexure-3 (contd.)

Details	HPU	Showroom	HO	Total	IT Ujjain	ASM Sanawad	AP Ujjain	Grand Total
Sales	91160684	93773746	39989330	224923760	224923760	199808621	-	438160579
Subsidy on Janata cloth	12667271	554028	8932	13230231	-	-	-	13230231
Misc. Income/ Receipts	130627	192497	316318	639442	63692	934096	18172	1655402
Interest Receipts	-	-	311806	311806	-	-	-	461039
Closing Stock	63080772	43440173	-	106520945	911915	11069750	-	118502610
IUT Sales	58868296	-	-	58868296	-	-	-	58868296
MDA Claim	-	-	6742986	6742986	-	-	-	6742986
Total	225907650	137960444	47369372	411237466	14403805	211961700	18172	637621143
Profit & Loss(-)	8235181	5719414	14208010	28162606	87991599	659399	79721	116934201
Income related to previous year	1909	-	40875	42784	78837	380972	-	502143
Expenses	31686	103429	137375	272490	-	379088	-	651578
Profit/Loss for the year (-)	8264958	5822843	14304510	28392311	87913212	657515	79721	117042759

Annexure-4

State-wise comparative financial performance of STCs for the year 1993-94

(Rs. in Lakhs)

Details	*Gujarat*	*Haryana*	*Jammu & Kashmir*	*Karna-taka*	*Kerala*	*Maha-rashtra*	*Orissa*	*Punjab*	*West Bengal*	*Madhya Pradesh*
Equity capital	264	254	300	-	458	4020	74	778	449	685.95
Accumulated losses	5	223	349	328	333	7364	5853	-	295	3915.12
Total revenue	263	692	766	387	572	10663	4745	824	2410	4458.21
Profit after tax	-	-37	-99	-	-75	351	-209	70	-	-1170.43

Annexure-5

PERFORMANCE OF OTHER STATE TEXTILE CORPORATION

Andhra Pradesh

The Andhra Pradesh Textile Development Corporation was set up in 1975, with its main objective being to promote, own, establish, aid and assist rehabilitation, growth and development of the handloom, powerloom and sericulture industry within and outside the cooperative fold. The corporation has eight production centres and five sales outlets. It has an equity capital of Rs. 438 lakhs. This corporation is ranked among the top ten profit-making SLPEs in the State. It has never declared a dividend. The corporation's net profit has substantially fallen from Rs. 15.14 lakhs in 1991-92 to Rs. 3.13 lakhs in 1992-93. It accumulated losses stood at Rs. 148.21 lakhs as at March 31, 1994. The corporation has not been able to support even 1.5% of the weaver community in the non-cooperative sector. Its accounts have not been audited since 1982-83. There is a move to wind up the corporation by selling the existing assets, and the amount so realized is proposed to be utilized for offering severance to the employees. The Government of Andhra Pradesh has been considering the suggestion of handing over the Janata scheme activity of the corporation to the State Handloom Department or the Andhra Pradesh Weavers' Cooperative Society. The Government proposes to immediately initiate action for disposal of the assets of the corporation and reduce further losses by implementing a lay-off/retrenchment scheme and also stopping of commercial activities. It also proposes to initiate action under Chapter III of Section 484 of the Companies Act, 1956, for virtual liquidation.

Bihar

The Bihar Textiles Corporation was set up in February 1978. The main aim of this unit was to encourgae cotton, woollen and polyester textile industries. The total investment has been Rs. 621.85 lakhs. This corporation had a total of five units by the end of 1989-90. The turnover of this corporation was Rs. 62.42 lakhs. It incurred a loss of Rs. 30.08 lakhs for the same year. The main reason for the loss is said to be shortage of working capital.

Gujarat

The Gujarat Textile Corporation was established in 1968 with the main objective of running composite and grey mill units and production of yarn and cloth. This corporation has three subsidiary companies. The total investment in the corporation was Rs. 26,009.71 lakhs in 1993-94. The accumulated losses of the corporation have been steadily increasing and stood at Rs. 39,717.08 lakhs in 1993-94. Thus, this corporation has been declared sick by BIFR on September 2, 1993.

4

Madhya Pradesh State Industries Corporation Limited

Introduction

Madhya Pradesh State Industries Corporation (MPSIC) is one of the oldest public sector undertakings in Madhya Pradesh. It was incorporated in 1961 with the objectives of:

(i) managing the public sector undertakings transferred by the State Government Departments as well as its own units; and

(ii) promoting joint industrial ventures with a view to blend private entrepreneurship with Government.

MPSIC has its Head Office at Bhopal and employs 106 persons. It has a Board of Directors and Chairman nominated by the State Government. The Managing Director is appointed by the Government. Usually, an officer from All-India Service cadre is posted as Managing Director.

It has a paid-up share capital of Rs. 1511.67 lakhs. Reserves and surplus amounted to Rs. 61.77 lakhs as on 31.3.1997. Outstanding loans stand at Rs. 1919 lakhs. The accumulated loss is Rs. 597.69 lakhs. It has 19 units of its own, manufacturing diverse products such as leather goods, engineering and fabricated items, ceramic and potteries wooden and steel furniture, telecom products, watches, sugar and alcohol. It has also promoted/assisted 13 joint ventures in the State.

The Corporation was making continuous profits until 1992-93. This was mainly due to the fact that the alcohol-manufacturing unit (Ratlam Alcohol and Carbon Dioxide Plant) was making substantial profits. However, decontrol of molasses and changes in the liquor policy reversed the trend and the unit started incurring huge losses, which affected the overall profitability of the Corporation. During 1996-97, as per the provisional accounts, the Corporation suffered a loss of Rs. 596 lakhs against a turnover of Rs. 2454.70 lakhs.

Units of MPSIC

Sugar Plants

Out of the 19 units of the Corporation, two are sugar mills, one is the alcohol manufacturing plant (RACP), and the balance belong to other categories. A list of the units with employee strength and accumulated profit/loss is given in Annexure I.

Out of the two sugar plants, Seth Govindaram Sugar Mills, Mahindpur, is closed and proposed to be liquidated as per BIFR directive. Action has already been initiated to dispose of the assets. The sale proceeds will be utilised for payment of dues to workers first, and the remaining amount will be utilised to meet other liabilities.

The other mill, i.e. Jaora Sugar Mills, Jaora has a crushing capacity of 1000 MT of cane per day, whereas the minimum viable capacity is around 2500 MT per day. The machinery is also very old. In order to make the unit viable, total modernisation and expansion of the plant with 2500 MT capacity per day with cogeneration facility is required. This will call for huge investment. Under the circumstances, it may be prudent to hand over/sell this unit to any of the successful cooperative societies or private parties in the sugar sector.

Alcohol Plant

Another major unit under MPSIC is the Ratlam Alcohol

and Carbon Dioxide Plant (RACP). This unit has been given on a management contact to S.G. Distilleries for 20 years with effect from 1.1.1997. As per the contract, S.G. Distilleries will give 31% of profits to MPSIC, subject to certain minimum guaranteed payments, which on an average works out to about Rs. 80 lakhs per annum for 20 years. This arrangement can be continued, since it guarantees certain payments to the Corporation for the next 20 years. Scope for review and enhancement of minimum guaranteed payments could be examined. Possibilities of selling the unit can be considered at the end of the contract period.

Other Units

The remaining 16 units fall under engineering, fabrication, ceramics and leather sectors. The products manufactured are not of specialised nature and these are generally produced in the small scale sector. Also, the plant and machinery in these units are very old and the operations, therefore, do not appear to be cost effective. Annexure II shows the profit and loss of all the units under MPSIC and MPSIC (H.O.) during the last five years. It can be seen that most of them are continuously incurring losses, and the losses have generally increased from year to year. Even in the case of a few profit-making units, it can be seen from the Annexure that the profits are very nominal and are also getting reduced. Only two units have made a nominal profit during 1996-97.

It may also be noted that these units inherited by the State at the time of merger of princely States, etc., are spread over a large number of districts of MP. Annexure III shows the map of MP State and the location of the various units. Controlling these small, uneconomic and dispersed units from MPSIC Head Office at Bhopal is not a worthwhile proposition. The total number of employees in these 16 units is only 634. Since these are really small-scale units, without any social or strategic implications, have old machinery, and are uneconomic, it is felt that they do not serve any useful purpose. It is, therefore, suggested that these units be wound up.

The employees could be paid their terminal benefits from the proceeds of sale of assets of these units as they are in prime locations in the various towns. However, it is difficult to hazard any guess about the likely sale value, which needs a detailed study. It is suggested that the entire assets be revalued by a competent agency before disposal to assess the possible income from sale, as well as liabilities of these units.

The data showing the financial position of the Corporation during the last five years is given in Annexure IV.

Joint Venture Units

The Corporation is also having 13 joint venture units under its fold. A list of these companies is given in Annexure V. Of these, three are in operation and the remaining are either under orders of winding up by BIFR or taken over by MPSIDC/MPFC. The investment pattern in the venturesis as follows:-

Investment of MPSIC	Rs. 692.12 lakhs
Investment of other promoters and associates	Rs. 1362.54 lakhs
Banks and financial institutions	Rs. 165.57 lakhs
Public	Rs. 1041.21 lakhs
Total investment	Rs. 326.44 lakhs

In addition, there is an unsecured loan taken by MPSIC to the tune of Rs. 8.30 lakhs. MPSIC has stood guarantee for Rs. 90 lakhs, and the State Government for Rs. 65 lakhs. With regard to winding up orders, appointment of official liquidator is in process, and in some cases appeals have been preferred. The guarantees issued by Government and MPSIC are likely to be invoked.

The dues of employees of the units facing liquidation have not yet been finalised. The amount required for this purpose will be substantial, but would be the primary responsibility of the joint sector company and not MPSIC or the Government of MP. Unless a detailed study is made, it is difficult to determine the exact amount required for this purpose. Eventually, all these units will have to be liquidated.

Financial Requirements

There are 106 employees in the Head Office of MPSIC. If all the units as well as joint ventures are sold, there is no need for MPSIC's office and all the employees will become redundant. The possibility of employing some of them in other public sector undertakings can be considered. If it is not possible, all of them may be given voluntary retirement benefits and the Corporation as a whole may be wound up.

The amount required for giving voluntary retirement benefits to employees of the Corporation as well as to the units will amount to Rs. 6135 lakhs, as per the following estimate which also has taken into account the possible increase in salary as per the Fifth Central Pay Commission recommendations which have reportedly been accepted by the Government of Madhya Pradesh.

Category	*No. of employees to be given VRS benefit*	*Estimated amount per person (Rs. In Lakhs)*	*Total amount (Rs. In Lakhs)*
Class I & II	68	5.00	425.00
Class III	325	4.00	1625.00
Class IV	644	3.00	2415.00
Others	1336	1.00	1670.00
Total	2373		6135.00

Besides the above, 20 employees will be entitled for pension benefits under the State Government Rules which requires about Rs. 2 lakhs per employee as capital value. Hence, a total amount of Rs. 40 lakhs has to be allocated for this purpose.

Also, the State Government had taken over the management of Jiwajirao Sugar Company, Dalauda, which is now under liquidation as proposed by BIFR. There are 45 employees under Class III and 161 persons as seasonal. These employees should also be given VRS benefits, which is estimated at Rs. 341 lakhs as per the proposed scheme.

Thus, the total financial requirement towards VRS and other benefits is estimated to be Rs. 6516 lakhs.

Discussion

Although the Corporation was set up with the objectives of managing some of the Government-owned companies which are mostly small scale units, and to accelerate the industrial development of the State by setting up its own new units as well as joint ventures based on private entrepreneurship, the Corporation could not fulfil these objectives. The Government of MP has set up the MP Small Industries Corporation as well as MP Finance Corporation which are also promoting the assisting small scale industries. There is thus an overlap of functions and more than one organisation is trying to serve the objective, and may be not too efficiently or economically. Also, with the establishment of MP State Industrial Development Corporation Limited and its accent on medium and large-scale industries, and the advent of the Small Industries Development Bank of India and commercial banks, MPSIC's role in the development of industries in the State has become nominal. The loss of the Corporation during 1996-97 alone is Rs. 693 lakhs, which has been met through budgetary support of the State Government, MPSIC is neither effectively fulfilling governmental nor any developmental objectives. The Corporation is also not playing any strategic role in the economic development of the State. An objective assessment of the situation would point towards the appropriate decision of winding up MPSIC.

On a scrutiny of the annual accounts of the Company, the following points can be noted:

(i) The loan from the State Government has increased from Rs. 282.82 lakhs in 1992-93 to Rs. 1019.50 lakhs in 1996-97. This shows that the company is mainly depending on the State Government for its existence.

(ii) It appears that the investment of Rs. 662.67 lakhs in 1996-97 is not yielding the desired returns.

(iii) There is drastic reduction in the turnover by 50% during 1996-97 when compared to the previous year, and the loss incurred by the Company was Rs. 692.65 lakhs.

(iv) The Company had made marginal profits only during the years 1994-95 and 1995-96 and that too because of the income from disinvestment.

As the performance of the Corporation is fast deteriorating, and the scope for revival is very remote, an early decision is warranted.

Highlights of the Voluntary Retirement Scheme (VRS)

Once a decision is taken to accept a voluntary retirement of a particular employee, the Corporation will make terminal payment on the basis of salary of the month previous to the date of decision as under:

(i) Ex-gratia payment on account of VRS compensation shall be the amount equivalent to two months' salary for each completed year of service. The payment for the part of the year shall be calculated on a pro-rata basis.

OR

Salary at the time of retirement multiplied by the balance period of service left before the date of his retirement or superannuation, i.e. the total salary for the remaining period of service upto the date of retirement.

The ex-gratia payment will be the lower of the above two options. However, provided that the maximum amount payable under the scheme shall not exceed Rs. 5.00 lakhs in case of each employee.

(ii) In addition to the payment under this scheme, the employee shall also be entitled for CPF, Gratuity, Pension, Superannuation and other statutory/lawful benefits as receivable under law. He/She shall also be entitled for encashment of Earned Leave on retirement as per prevailing service rules.

(iii) Three months' notice pay as per the conditions of service rules applicable to the employees.

(iv) Travel and transport expenses for self and family and household effects for proceeding to home-town or to the place where he/she intends to settle in India as per the entitlement under the TA rules of the Corporation.

The detailed Voluntary Retirement Scheme is enclosed in Annexure VI.

Conclusion

Viewed from any angle, the prospects of MPSIC are very bleak. There is no possibility of the units of MPSIC being taken over by any other Corporation of the Government of MP including MPFC. It is, therefore, recommended that the activities of MPSIC be stopped forthwith and the Corporation and its units be wound up. A Voluntary Retirement Scheme is proposed (given in Annexure VI). The employees may be given VRS benefits as per the scheme.

Action Plan

The following action plan consisting of major activities is recommended:

(i) Action may be taken to complete up to date audit of accounts, especially in the units.

(ii) Finalise a suitable Voluntary Retirement Scheme for the employees at the Head Office of MPSIC and the units. (A draft scheme is given in Annexure VI).

(iii) Get the assets revalued by an accredited agency.

(iv) All the assets of the Corporation may be sold through a tender-cum-auction process.

(v) Depending upon the realisations, all liabilities of the Corporation should be liquidated from the sale proceeds including the terminal benefits to employees.

(vi) Action may be initiated for winding up of the Corporation after getting due clearances from the Government, institutions and other creditors.

(vii) Arrangements for a core group of employees and agency to undertake the orderly winding up within a definite time-frame may be made.

Implementation Schedule

PERT Chart

A PERT chart indicating the various activities and the estimated duration of each activity is given in Annexure VII. It can be seen that the entire work is to be completed within a period of 56 weeks. Therefore, the winding up process can be completed in a time-frame of little more than one year from the time of final decision to close down the Corporation.

Annexure-6

Madhya Pradesh Industries Corporation Limited Voluntary Retirement Scheme (VRS - 98)

Preamble — To rationalise its operations and reduce the existing strength of employees, M.P. State Industries Corporation Limited (MPSIC) is launching a Voluntary Retirement Scheme.

Definition

VRS-98 Scheme — The scheme will be called MPSIC Voluntary Retirement Scheme, 1998.

Employees — Means MPSIC cadre employee by whatever name called including workers and executive (excluding temporary/daily wage/contingency paid employees).

Management — Means Board of Directors of MPSIC or Managing Director or a committee constituted by the Board.

Year — Means Financial Year

Retirement — Means 58 years of age or as per amendment prevailing as per Service Rules of the Corporation.

Salary — Means Basic Pay + D.A. + I.R. + C.C.A.

Scheme

This scheme will be applicable to all employees (in whatever name called) including workers and executives (excluding temporary/daily wage/contingency paid employees) of MPSIC and also employees who have been taken in cadre of MPSIC by virtue of transfer/absorbed from other Corporation or the State Government.

Eligibility — All employees who have completed 10

	years of service or completed 40 years of the age as on the date of notification by the Corporation.
Mode of Operation	VRS-98 will remain open for receiving applications from the employees within two months from the date of notification.
Tax Benefit	The Scheme will be exempted from Income Tax within the parameters of Section 10(10)(c) of the Income Tax Act, 1961 and Rule 2BA of Income Tax Rules, 1992.
Scheme	1. All eligible employees are allowed to give option within the period of validity of the Scheme. The management will have right not to grant voluntary retirement for reasons, which are to be recorded in writing.
	2. Once option is given by an employee it cannot be changed.
	3. Once the management decides to allow retirement to the employee and settle the account, the employee can not be employed on contract or otherwise in the service of MPSIC or any of its subsidiaries/joint venture companies.
	4. After the payment is settled and paid to the employee, he/she cannot claim any more amount under the scheme except his/her legitimate claims like PF, Gratuity, Pension etc. He/She is also not entitled for any medical, conveyance, housing and any other facilities or benefits in future.

5. All previous dues of employees such as loans, other advances etc., will be settled against the amount payable under the scheme.

6. Once a decision is taken to accept a Voluntary Retirement of a particular employees, Corporation will make terminal payment on the basis of salary of the month previous to the date of decision as under:

(i) Ex-gratia payment on account of VRS compensation shall be the amount equivalent to two months' salary for each completed year of service. The payment for the part of the year shall be calculated on pro-rata basis.

Or

Salary at the time of retirement multiplied by the balance period of service left before the date of his retirement or superannuation i.e. the total salary for the remaining period of service upto the date of retirement.

The payment will be the lower of the above two options. However, provided that the maximum amount payable under the scheme shall not exceed Rs. 5.00 lakhs in case of each employee.

(ii) In addition to the payment under this scheme, the employee shall also be entitled for CPF, Gratuity, Pension superannuation and other statutory/ lawful benefits as receivable per law. He/She shall also be entitled for encashment of Earned Leave on retirement as per prevailing Service Rules.

(iii) Three months' notice pay as per the condition of service rules applicable to the employees.

(iv) Travel and transport expenses for self and family and household for proceeding to home-town or to the place where he intends to settle in India as per his entitlement under the TA rules of the Corporation.

7. The vacancy in the post caused by the voluntary retirement is not to be filled up by new recruitment on contract or otherwise. The vacancy, however, can be filled up by promotion as per rules. The purpose of VRS-98 is to result in overall reduction in the existing strength of employees.

8. The employee(s) opting for VRS is/are required to vacate the houses allotted to them and/or the housing facilities provided will be withdrawn after a period of two months.

9. All claims under this scheme and other retirement benefits shall be released on or before the date employee is relieved from the service of the Corporation.

General

1. The amount of VRS will be subject to TDS as per the provisions of Income Tax and rules prevailing at the time of settlement.

2. The cut-off month will be taken as the month in which decision allowing

Voluntary Retirement is communicated.

3. In case of any dispute regarding interpretation in implementation of rules, terms and conditions, the decision of the management shall be final and binding to all concerned.

4. Any legal matter will be subject to MP jurisdiction only.

5

Madhya Pradesh State Mining Corporation Limited

Introduction

Madhya Pradesh State Mining Corporation (MPSMC) is a wholly-owned public sector undertaking of the Government of Madhya Pradesh. It was incorporated in the year 1962 and function under the administrative control of the Department of Mineral Resources and Tourism of the Government of Madhya Pradesh.

The Memorandum of Association of MPSMC lists the following as the objectives of the Corporation:

- To search for major and minor minerals and precious stones in the State of MP and to acquire, by purchase or grant, mining and other rights in the lands within the State of MP.
- To acquire by purchase or otherwise, ores or mineral produce, for the purpose of working and rendering the same marketable, and selling and disposing of the same.
- To acquire mining rights by obtaining licences/leases from the Government.
- To apply for purchase or otherwise acquire any patents, licences and like rights.

- To carry on trading in minerals by acting as intermediaries between the State Trading Corporation and the mine-owner.
- To provide facilities for transportation of such major and minor minerals, the development of which will directly benefit the Corporation.
- To carry on the search for mining, getting, obtaining, cutting, polishing and dealing in all precious, semi-precious and valuable stones.
- To provide funds for the purpose of prospecting, investigating and experimenting to any company, firm or person with a view to furthering any or all of the objectives of the Company.
- To adopt such means of making known the products of the Company as may seem expedient.
- To do all or any of the above things, and all such other things, as are incidental or conductive to the attainment of the above objectives.

In view of the large mineral resource base of the State, and the likelihood of the discovery of diamonds and other gems, precious metals and some high-grade minerals, the Government wishes to exercise close control over MPSMC. The Government would like to use MPSMC as its agent, as well as policy instrument, for mineral resource exploitation, particularly because minerals are non-renewable, depleting assets. Moreover, the Government of India's policy of fixing royalty on minerals found in the State is not considered equitable from the point of view of the State Government. The State Government also appears to be sensitive about the recent developments and controversies surrounding the grant of licences for diamond exploration.

Staff

The total number of personnel as on December 1, 1997 was 932, comprising of 19 Managerial, 906 Non-Managerial, and 7 Contract Staff. Due to withdrawal from some activities, the Corporation recently reduced its labour strength by approximately 2400 persons on payment of retrenchment compensation. MPSMC is of the view that they still have to shed some surplus workers and are now contemplating a Voluntary Retirement Scheme to right-size the organization.

Organizational Set Up

The powers of direction, superintendence and control of the Company is vested in the Board of Directors, but is subject to overall directives from the Government of Madhya Pradesh. The Chairman and the Managing Director, who is the Chief Executive Officer, and other Directors, are appointd by the government. The part-time, non-executive Chairman of the Corporation is the Minister in Charge of the Department. The Principal Secretary to the Government of Madhya Pradesh in the Mineral Resources Department is the Managing Director.

Need for Distancing MPSMC from Government

The appointment of both the Chairman and Managing Director, who are Government functionaries, may not be an appropriate arrangement from the tents of corporate governance, functional and operational autonomy. The arrangement detracts from the ideal functioning of a corporate entity as well as assessment of the performance of the Corporation. Both the Chairman and the Managing Director, being drawn from the Government makes the Corporation a virtual extension of, and instrument of the Government, and may not be exactly conducive to a level playing field concept or autonomous functioning of MPSMC as a Board-managed company. If, for policy reasons, the Chairman has to be from Government, at least the Managing Director ought to be a qualified, full-time employee of the Corporation. Distancing the MPSMC from the Government should receive priority attention.

Professional Expertise Needed

The Board of a Mining Company should provide for

appropriate representation and assemblage of relevant expertise of mining, exploration, finance, legal, technological and other professional skills which could speed up the mineral exploration and exploitation process and industrial development of Madhya Pradesh. MPSMC should endeavour to add economic and market value, create mining infrastructure and help generate employment opportunities and incomes for economically depressed people in remote, hilly and forest areas, with due regard to ecology, which calls for requisite Board-level expertise, as well as professional supporting staff.

Board of Directors

The number of the members in the Board of Directors varies from year to year. In the year 1996-97, the Board of Directors was constituted with ten Government Officials and seven politicians. The tenure of the nominee Board members from Government is coterminus with the office of the officials. The non-officials are allowed a two-year term. There are very frequent changes in CEOs and other functional directors. Although hardly three or four meetings of the Board are held in a year, only three to four members attend. Details of meetings of the Board of Directors are presented below, which is self-explanatory.

Meetings of the Board of Directors

Year	*1992-93*	*1993-94*	*1994-95*	*1995-96*	*1996-97*
No. of Directors	14	11	16	12	17
No. of Meetings held	4	7	5	5	6
No. of Directors who attended the Annual General Meeting	3	3	3	3	4

Remuneration

The executives and staff in the Corporation are appointed by the Chief Executive Officer in accordance with the rules and guidelines set by the Board. The pay scales in the Corporation follow the pattern set by Government for public sector corporations. The pay scales are not able to attract people of requisite calibre and competence. Remuneration of top executives if fixed in line with private sector and industry norms will help MPSMC to attract and retain talent.

Restructuring Necessary

The organizational structure of the Corporation and calibre of personnel is not such as to be able to cope with the task of fulfilling the objectives that have been assigned to it. Restructuring the Corporation is recommended to equip and enable it to competently amd effectively to achieve its objectives. This exercise should commence with the Board of Directors.

Reconstitution of the Board

The Board should be reconstituted with requisite professionally qualified and experienced people. It should have a mix of professionals, Government nominees and men of public standing, and be headed by an experienced non-executive Chairman with the required background of exploration, exploitation and techno-economic evaluation. The Board should have functional Directors in charge of Prospecting and Geology, Mining and Production, Processing and Marketing, and Finance. The professional component should include mining engineers, geologists, financial and marketing experts, economists, and personnel experts. Association of CEOs from reputed central and state public sector mining companies will help in upgrading policy formulation and skill-development.

Government Control

The Government decides allotment of leases to MPSMC. Senior level appointments in MPSMC are made by the Committee constituted by the Department of Public Enterprises of the Government of Madhya Pradesh. Government ratification is reqquired for incurring capital expenditure above Rs. 25 lakhs. The Board is competent to take decisions on matters regarding collaborations. Decisions with regard to pricing, investment, hiring of labour, settlement and suspensions are taken by the CEO. According to the MPSMC grapevine, politicians tend to canvass for appointments and transfers, and for lucrative commercial opportunities, while Government officials do not take much interest in the matters of the Corporation. The Government monitors the functioning of the enterprise through an annual performance contract called Memorandum of Understanding (MOU) every year. There is scope for improvement in the criteria and evaluation of performance of the Corporation through the MOU.

Mineral Resources of Madhya Pradesh

Madhya Pradesh is a major mineral producing State of the country. It is endowed with large deposits of coal, bauxite, copper, limestone, dolomite, iron ore, phosphorite, manganese ore and minor minerals. It is the only diamond producing State in India at present. The value of minerals produced in the State during the year 1993-94 was estimated at Rs. 3424 crore and Rs. 4400 crore in 1996-97. The State continues to retain the third position in the country, and accounts for 12% of the total value of minerals produced in the country. Mineral revenue has increased from Rs. 0.81 crore in 1956-57 to Rs. 847.76 crore in 1996-97, indicating the scope for future development. MP's share in total value of minerals produced in the country works out to about 24% if crude oil, petroleum and natural gas are excluded.

The Business Profile of MPSMC

MPSMC has been involved in mining of some major and minor minerals. The current break-up of business of MPSMC for the year 1996-97 is given in the Table 5.1.

Table 5.1

S. No.	*Mineral*	*Percentage*
1.	Rock phosphate	48.48
2.	Sand	30.43
3.	Bauxite	6.61
4.	Dolomite	6.10
5.	Corundum	3.31
6.	Tin ore	2.47

It may be noted that MPSMC is not yet a major player or even stakeholder in several important industrial minerals though there is good scope. The only mineral in which it has an effective stake is the mining and beneficiation of rock phosphate. Unless the Corporation builds itself up to undertake activities, which add value to mineral production, it may not be able to achieve its objectives.

Main Features of Financial Position

The authorized capital of the Company is Rs. 5 crore, while the paid-up capital is Rs. 2.19 crore. The Company has not taken any loans and, therefore, no capital gearing exists. Such a gearing could increase the earning per share of the Corporation considerably.

The application of funds is skewed in favour of working capital. As against the net block of Rs. 2.72 crore in 1996-97, the investment in current assets was Rs. 17.50 crore. The investment in working capital was Rs. 15.44 crore, and the turnover of inventory was 3:1 in 1996-97. The turnover of cash and bank balance was also of the same order during the year. The turnover of loans and advances was 5:1. This shows that the funds did not rotate fast enough in these components of working capital, and they suffered from a surfeit of investment. In 1996-97, the funds raised through current liabilities were minimal and turned out to be about 10% of the current assets.

The Corporation earned profits during 1995-96 and 1996-97. However, the profits turned out to be a very small fraction of the total turnover. For instance, in 1996-97, the profits were a mere 1.6% of the total turnover. During 1994-95, the Company incurred a loss of Rs. 1.16 crore. One of the reasons for low profits in 1996-97 was the high incidence of expenses incurred on mining and prospecting. The selling expenses were roughly about 20% of the turnover, and the expenses incurred on employee remuneration and facilities were about 30% of the turnover. The income statement for the years 1994-95 and 1995-96 reveals that the expenses incurred under mining and prospecting and employee remuneration and facilities were roughly of the same proportion during these two years.

Future Prospects

Madhya Pradesh is endowed with good mineral resources, and is the third largest mineral producing State in India. The value of mineral production in the year 1993-94 was Rs. 3424 crore, representing 12% of the value of mineral production in India. The value of mineral production in Madhya Pradesh has registered good progress in recent years and stood at Rs. 4400 crore. The State has large deposits of important minerals like bauxite, coal, copper, dolomite, limestone, manganese ore, phosphorite, barytes, tin and corundum. It is the only producer of diamonds in the country at Panna. There are propsects of discovery of certain strategic and rare minerals like titanium, tungsten and beryllium. There are good prospects of discovery of gold and other precious metals. Kimberlite pipes have also been discovered in several districts, indicating the presence of diamonds. There has been good response from multinational and Indian companies for exploration and exploitation of diamonds in the State in response to the recent tender floated by the Government of Madhya Pradesh.

Industrial minerals provide good opportunities for development of industry in the Mine-Mineral-Metal-Material value chain. There are good prospects for development of iron and steel, aluminium, copper, cement, ferro-chrome, fertilizer, chemical and other mineral-based industries in the State. However, it would appear that the Government of Madhya Pradesh and MPSMC have not been able to promote adequate interest and investment in exploration and mining of minerals and setting up of mineral-based industries. Worldover there is greater emphasis on both surface and underground exploration through closely-spaced aeromagnetic and radiometric surveys. Such surveys zero in on prospective areas where detailed exploration and drilling activities can prove the existence of mines, and the economic viability of mining operations. There is also a need to shift from technology-oriented metallurgical knowledge to science-oriented new material sciences, which can lead to higher value addition. This calls for better R&D efforts and good linkages between R&D institutions, industry and mining. MPSMC and the State Government could usefully tap the expertise and facilities of the Regional Research Laboratory at Bhopal.

There is a need for MPSMC to reposition itself to secure maximum spatial spread of growth and benefit percolation to the less-advantaged population. MPSMC has to review the Memorandum of Association and its Articles in the light of the present needs of intensifying exploratory work, sourcing of technology, building up of skills and ensuring proper conditions for rapid growth of the mineral-based industry in the State. MPSMC would be well-advised to review its strategies and prepare a corporate plan which fulfils the aims of the Government and the objectives of the Corporation. Such an exercise would have to commence with a Resource Audit of the mineral resources in the State and delineate the role and responsibility of MPSMC. As the National Mineral Policy permits only 50% equity to be held by foreign parties in an Indian company engaged in mining activities, MPSMC should position itself to promote suitable joint ventures with Indian and foreign parties. MPSMC could actively seek mining rights from the State Government and convert them into leases, and use such leases as an instrument for leveraging further investments and promoting joint ventures.

MPSMC would have to undertake pre-investment feasibility reports and develop technology-scanning systems to source technologies for value addition and commercial marketing of intermediaries and finished products. It would also have to develop feasibility reports to persuade investors to invest in Madhya Pradesh. Suitable escort services should also be provided. MPSMC should be given adequate powers to incur capital expenditure of upto Rs. 5 crore without reference to the Government. MPSMC would have to be adequately professionalised and given requisite autonomy and financial powers to be able to channelise investment for exploration, exploitation, benefaction and utilization of mineral resources to sustain a vibrant mineral industry in the State. The Government of Madhya Pradesh should accord MPSMC a better status on the analogy of a *Schedule A* company of the Government of India. If properly manned and led, MPSMC can bid to become a pioneer and strong player in the mineral development of the State. The Government of Madhya Pradesh would also be in a better position to utilize MPSMC to advise it in regard to mineral development in the State, including appropriate regulatory, marketing and tax policies, which could help accelerate the economic development of the State.

Recommendation

MPSMC has a net worth of Rs. 763.49 lakhs. Its capital structure has to be strengthened, positive image created, corporate plans prepared, and functioning professionalised to secure loan funds and undertake technically feasible, economically viable and financially sound projects for execution on its own, or in collaboration with other partners. Given its present level of functioning and limitations, there is scope for partnerships, alliances and linkages. Strategic partners, if inducted, could make MPSMC a real instrument and catalyst for mineral and economic development of Madhya Pradesh.

The Government of Madhya Pradesh has accorded priority to exploration, exploitation of natural resources and technological development. It considers the mining sector as a core and crucial sector, both from the point of view of industrial development, balanced regional development, provision of jobs to economically weaker sections, and protection of the ecology. MPSMC could prove to be a useful instrument of the Government to ensure proper and competitive development of the mineral and the mineral-based industry in the State. It could also help the State Government to garner some sweat equity and supplement its royalty income, provided the necessary homework is done and a level playing field is created.

In view of the strategic importance of MPSMC in the exploration of mineral resources and mineral development of the State, there is a good case for retaining substantial State ownership of MPSMC in accordance with the present Government policy and restructuring it to fulfil the recent State Government objectives. If MPSMC is unable to attract good talent on the Board, and retain professional skills, Government should consider the possibility of inducting strategic partners with substantial equity to enhance the strengths, dynamism and vitality of the Corporation. MPSMC should position itself strategically with a clear focus and proper mandate. This could be done by inducting successful public sector, joint sector or transnational companies as joint venture partners in MPSMC, or any other joint ventures or subsidiaries of MPSMC.

6

Madhya Pradesh Housing Board

Introduction

In a developing country like India with ever-growing population, the problem of housing shortage is endemic and acute. According to a survey by the National Building Organization (NBO), the housing shortage in India as of 1991 was 22.66 million units, i.e. 14.55 million units in rural and 8.11 million units in urban areas. The overall shortage in the country during the decade has only marginally reduced from 23.27 million units in 1981 to 22.66 million units in 1991. While the shortage has come down from 16.29 million units in rural areas in 1981 to 14.55 in 1991, the shortage in urban areas went up from 6.98 million units in 1981 to 8.11 million units in 1991. In the State of Madhya Pradesh, however, the overall shortage remained static at 0.84 million units. While the shortage in rural areas has come down from 0.57 to 0.44 million units, the urban shortage has increased from 0.275 to 0.40 million units.

National Housing Policy

The National Housing Policy envisages the role of housing agencies as one of facilitators and promoters in housing and urban development as part of the economic reforms undertaken by the Government. The National as well as the State-level Housing Policies perceive the Government's new role as that of an 'ENABLER' rather than a 'PROVIDER' of all resources and services. It is also visualized that the

Government will devise and implement strategies which enable the various agencies to complement the efforts of one another to ensure most efficient utilization of resources in line with demand.

State Housing Boards

India's State Housing Boards are the main providers of Government-sponsored housing schemes to meet the ever-growing paucity of housing in almost all the States. The housing agencies have largely been guided by an "Engineering Approach" aimed at sheer output of maximum number of dwelling units, while they have no influence on the overall housing process. This has been the case for the last 30 years or so. Housing Boards have been entrusted with Government funds to address the country's housing problems. In the 1960s when most of the Housing Boards were established, this coincided with the emergence of the concept of Economically Weaker Sections (EWS) of Society. However, only after the establishment of the Housing and Urban Development Corporation (HUDCO) in 1970 did the Housing Boards actually take off. This was done by:

- firm establishment of institutional housing finance arrangements; and
- launching of a variety of programmes such as EWS, LIG (Low Income Group), MIG (Middle Income Group) schemes, Cooperative Housing, Staff Housing, Group Housing, Rental Housing, Rural Housing Schemes, etc., meant for different target groups.

MP Housing Board and Composition

The MP Housing Board (MPHB) was established in the year 1972 under MP Griha Nirman Mandal Adhiniyam, 1972, which replaced the MP Housing Board Act of 1950. It is governed by a Board of Directors consisting of a Chairman and a Vice-Chairman appointed by the State Government. The Housing Commissioner to the Board is the principal executive officer of the Board under the overall control of the Board and the Chairman. The State Government appoints the Housing Commissioner and the Board of Directors representing Housing, Finance, Revenue, Rural Development, and Town and Country Planning Departments, two Members of the Legislative Assembly, two experts, and two non-official members. The Housing Commissioner is the Member-Secretary. The Board may appoint a Chief Engineer, a Chief Accounts Officer, an Estate Manager, and such other officers as it considers necessary.

Organizational Structure

At the field-level, there are four Zones headed by Additional Housing Commissioners located at Bhopal, Indore, Raipur and Jabalpur. There are ten Circle Offices headed by Deputy Housing Commissioners, two located at Bhopal, one each at Gwalior, Indore, Ujjain, Jabalpur, Rewa, Sagar, Durg and Raipur. In addition, there are 32 Divisional Offices headed by Executive Engineers and 80 Sub-Divisional Offices spread over the entire State.

Objectives

The objectives of MPHB are:

- To provide houses and to develop housing sites along with related facilities such as office complexes and commercial areas.
- Accord priority to economically weaker sections and disadvantaged groups for effective solution of the housing problem.
- Encourage NGOs (Non-Governmental Organizations), private builders and cooperative housing societies to provide housing.

Functions

The principal activity of the Housing Board is to provide houses and develop housing sites for the people, along with related facilities such as office complexes and commercial areas. The Board carries out these activities through the mechanisms of:

- Self-finance;
- Hire purchase; and
- Deposit works.

Over the years, the Board has also had to undertake maintenance activities of various properties developed by it. The Board has increasingly been carrying out deposit works for various Government Departments, and now intends to venture into infrastructure development activities also.

Institutional finance is obtained from national-level instituitions such as HUDCO, NHB, CANFIN HOMES, CENT BANK, HDFC, etc.

Personnel

The Housing Board has 3823 employees, of whom 1066 are engineering staff and 2757 administrative staff. The details are given in Annexure-I. In view of the surplus staff, uncertainties of funds and works, and increased competition, there is a proposal to prune the staff strength by 1700. The Voluntary Retirement Scheme (VRS) is expected to cost MPHB around Rs. 24.40 crores, details of which are furnished under the head "VOLUNTARY RETIREMENT SCHEME".

Current Activities

MPHB is the main institutional instrument of the State Government for the implementation of the New Housing Policy. Providing houses and developing house plots is the chief activity of MPHB.

Urban Housing

MPHB has taken up construction of commercial complexes not only as income-generating projects, but also as an instrument for augmenting public convenience and increasing the beauty of the urban landscape. A project to construct 2000 small shops in various Housing Board Colonies around the State has been visualized.

The Board has decided to construct poly-clinic complexes on self-finance basis, which will consist of poly-clinics, doctors' chambers, operation theatres, x-ray/pathology centres, nursing homes, cafeterias, and residential flats for the doctors and allied service personnel.

A pilot project for the construction of 2500 houses for "hamals" (head-load workers) at various places in the State is to be implemented with financial assistance from HUDCO.

The Board has signed an MOU with the MP Karmachari Awas Nigam to construct houses/develop plots for Government employees in various District and Tehsil headquarters of the State. The Board proposes to augment Government housing through re-densification efforts in all the major towns of the State.

Infrastructural Schemes

In the New Housing Policy, MPHB has been given the additional option for execution of infrastructural schemes in the State. The Board is expected to undertake construction of bridges on rivers, major roads, including State/national highways, schemes for water supply and sewerage in the big towns, etc., by arranging institutional finance. MPHB will be free to impose toll tax on the services to repay loans.

Awas Vikas Sansthan

Awas Vikas Sansthan (AVS) is a registered society promoted by the Housing Board, and is a State-level apex body established for creating a network of Building Centres in Madhya Pradesh. It is a "No Profit-No loss" agency devoted to skill upgradation and production of low-cost, locally-available and effective building materials.

So far, Building Centres have been sanctioned to AVS by HUDCO. These Centres are imparting training to masons, plumbers, carpenters, etc., through schemes like NRY training programme, etc. AVS has conducted training programmes for engineers also and recently started a unique scheme of "Earn While You Learn". Unemployed educated youth (technical as well as non-technical) are imparted training in the production of cost-effective building materials. These components are marketed by the centres for various housing projects at pre-determined rates. The trainee entrepreneur is able to earn, on an average Rs. 3000 to Rs. 5000 per month.

Other Major Projects

MPHB has developed a scheme for satellite townships at Bhopal, Gwalior (Maharajpur) and Sagar. They have also taken up the re-densification of MOG Lines at Indore at an estimated cost of Rs. 40 crores. To meet the housing needs of the steel industries, a new township is being developed in different categories have been completed.

Deposit Works

In addition to its housing activities, MPHB is also executing works for various departments as deposit works. The works are of Reserve Bank of India, Bank of India, Bhabha Atomic Research Centre, the Departments of Tribal Welfare, Police, Education, Technical Education and Local Self-Government, Employee State Insurance Corporation, Kendriya Vidyalaya, Navodaya Vidyalaya, Indian Airlines, and varaious other Departments. Buildings ranging from offices to hospitals, colleges, schools, bus stands and hotels have been built.

Buildings of the Director, Technical Education, under the World Bank aided schemes are being constructed at several places. The Board is also entrusted with the construction of Navodaya Vidyalayas in various districts of Madhya Pradesh. The total cost of these works is Rs. 34 crores. The Board is executing works of the Tribal Welfare Department at 1446 places in the State costing Rs. 84 crores. The Board is also carrying out a prestigious project for the Dr. Ambedkar Natioal Institute at Mhow.

Deposit works costing more than Rs. 230 crores have

already been completed and works of about Rs. 34 crores are in progress.

Physical Performance

A detailed account of houses completed and plots developed by MPHB for the last four years is appended vide Annexure-II (histogram).

Houses

The actual achievement in respect of targets of houses to be built has come down from 89.6% in 1993-94 to 68.6% in 1994-95, 67.2% in 1995-96, and to 69% in 1996-97. Evidently, the actual achievement is far below the target and is below 70%, except in 1993-94 when it was 89.6%. The histogram annexed gives the position.

Developed Plots

Similarly, the actual development of plots against the target is also not very encouraging. It was 85.4% in 1993-94, which has come down to 83% in 1994-95, 63% in 1995-96, and 58.6% in 1996-97. There is a gradual decline from 1993-94 onwards. The annexed histogram may be seen. There is an urgent need to arrest the deteriorating trend and show better achievements against the targets fixed both in regard to houses constructed and plots developed.

Problems and Prospects

The record of repayment of loans taken by MPHB is quite good as it has never defaulted in payments of instalments. It is, however, plagued by three major problems:

1. It has unsold property worth about Rs. 60 crores spread across various parts of the state. It is partly due to projects being taken up in the past without proper assessment of demand and the pactice of the Housing Board by which old properties are not depreciated but interest is added on. They are trying to correct this by:

(i) Not beginning construction of any project without collecting at least 50% registration charges; and

(ii) Coming out with attractive schemes whereby concessions in accrued interest are given so as to encourage sale of unsold property.

2. An amount of over Rs. 40 crores is oerdue from various beneficiaries. Limited concessions are being extended in respect of penal interest to encourage repayment of overdue loans.

3. Another major problem faced by the Board is the decision of the Revenue Board of the Government of Madhya Pradesh to make the Housing Board liable to pay Land Diversion Tax which is a tax levied for diversion of land from agricultural purposes to construction activity. District Collectors have raised demands amounting to over Rs. 10 crores. The Board is unable to recover this amount from past beneficiaries who had purchased land and houses during the last 25 years. Government could consider waiving this sum, while MPHB could build this amount into their costing of construction and site development for the future from an agreed cut-off date.

The major challenge is a better, more cost-effective, competitive and speedy implementation of the Government's New Housing Policy. For this purpose, they could collaborate with private parties, housing cooperative societies, private architects, planners and builders. MPHB could play a catalytic role in increasing awareness and use of locally-available low-cost, environment-friendly building materials and techniques.

To reach of MPHB in the rural areas is not adequate and needs to be extended while being cost-effective. This could be done by improving the professional competence and appropriately expanding the network in the rural sector through partnerships, alliances and linkages. The basic infrastructure and capacity exists with MPHB to undertake the additional workload and enhance the operational arena, and take advantage of new opportunities.

Sources of Finance

MPHB obtains funds from various sources as detailed vide Annexure-III.

The main sources of finance for MPHB include secured loans, unsecured loans, sale of houses and plots, deposits, etc. Secured loans include debentures, loans from banks, loans from MPHB (WBP), loans from HUDCO, LIC, GIC, NHB, HDFC, World Bank, etc. The unsecured loans include loans from Government, financial institutions, public, etc.

The amount of secured loans outstanding as on March 31, 1993 was Rs. 11276 lakhs, which increased to Rs. 14573 lakhs in 1993-94, to Rs. 15893 lakhs in 1994-95, to Rs. 16660 lakhs in 1995-96 and to Rs.20526 lakhs in 1996-97. Among the secured loans category, the maximum contribution was in the form of loans from HUDCO, followed by loans from other institutions and debentures.

The amount of unsecured loans outstanding was Rs. 2042 lakhs in 1992-93, which came down to Rs. 1864 lakhs in 1993-94, before increasing gradually to Rs. 2069 lakhs in 1996-97. The major contribution under unsecured loans category was in the form of loans from Government, followed by loans from financial institutions. The amount of loans borrowed from the public was a meagre Rs. 1.04 lakhs. It is surprising that this source is not tapped to its full potential. If good credit rating is obtained, there will be ample scope for mobilizing funds through public deposits.

The amount mobilized through sale of houses/plots was Rs. 2984 lakhs in 1993-94, which increased to Rs. 3132 lakhs in 1993-94, and to Rs. 10121 lakhs in 1994-95. Later, it drastically came down to Rs. 4385 lakhs in 1995-96, and to Rs. 2830 lakhs in 1996-97. The reasons for this downward trend have to be identified and steps taken for immediate sale of already constructed houses or developed plots.

Important Financial Indicators

The important financial indicators of MPHB are indicated vide Annexure-IV.

The total revenue from sale of houses/plots was Rs. 2984 lakhs in 1992-93, which increased to Rs. 3132 in 1993-94. There was substantial increase in the revenue from sale of houses/plots in 1994-95, i.e. Rs. 10121 lakhs. It decreased to Rs. 4385 lakhs in 1995-96, and to Rs. 2830 lakhs in 1996-97. The reasons have to be ascertained for this gradual fall in revenue, and steps taken to dispose of the developed plots or constructed houses. It is also observed that cost of sales as a percentage of revenue from sale of houses/plots is very high. There is an urgent need to reduce the cost of sales substantially, which will go a long way in improving the profitability of the organization.

The gross profit of MPHB, which was Rs. 155.41 lakhs in 1992-93, increased to Rs. 264.36 lakhs in 1993-94, and to Rs. 530.70 lakhs in 1994-95. It was Rs. 464.07 lakhs in 1995-96, and decreased to Rs. 363.05 lakhs in 1996-97. The gross profit margin also shows an increasing trend over the period.

The net profit which was Rs. 142.09 lakhs in 1992-93, decreased to Rs. 55.86 lakhs in 1993-94. It went up to Rs. 151.63 lakhs in 1994-95, came down to Rs. 81.37 lakhs in 1995.96, and was at Rs.70.08 lakhs in 1996-97. The decline in net profit may be attributed to increasing interest costs and establishment expenses. This is also evident from the net profit margins calculated for the given period. The net profit margin which was 4.76% in 1992-93, decreased to 1.50% in 1994-95, and then slightly increased to 2.48% in 1996-97. Hence, there is an urgent need to cut down the establishment expenses and interest obligations. Since dependence on debt-sources involves fixed interest obligations, the option to increase equity may be explored.

The current ratio which was 1.45 in 1992-93 gradually increased and stabilized at 1.57 in 1996-97. This testifies to the sound liquidity position of MPHB.

Status of Recovery

The following Table 5.2 shows the recovery of dues from hire purchase debtors for the last four years and accumulated dues:

Table 5.2
Recovery of Dues

(Rs. in lakhs)

Year	*Dues upto last year*	*Dues during the year*	*Total dues*	*Collected during the year*	*Recovery percentage*	*Balance dues (accumulated dues)*
1992-93	4779.25	386.01	5165.2	349.55	6.76%	4815.71
1993-94	4815.71	520.92	5336.6	655.82	12.29%	4680.81
1994-95	4680.81	2216.51	6897.3	708.49	10.27%	6188.83
1995-96	6188.83	539.73	6728.5	1176.44	17.48%	5552.12

Note: 1996-97 figures are not made available.

The total dues have been increasing from year to year. The amount increased from Rs. 5165.2 lakhs in 1992-93 to Rs. 6728.5 lakhs in 1995-96. The percentage of recovery of dues is very low and not at all encouraging.

Though there has been some improvement in recovery of dues from Rs. 349.55 lakhs in 1992-93 to Rs. 1176.44 lakhs in 1995-96, this is not at all a satisfactory position. The accumulated dues are large and represent poor financial management. Although some ad hoc special drives were launched, more concerted efforts and effective steps are needed to substantially reduce the accumulated dues.

Establishment Expenditure

There has been a continuous escalation in establishment expenditure from 16% in 1993-94 to 23% in 1994-95, 28% in 1995-96, and 23% in 1996-97. This continuous rise is reported to be due to increase in dearness allowances, increase of annual increments, implementation of new pay scales, etc. It appears that efforts to reduce unproductive manpower have not been adequate. The scope for farming out work and keeping only core technical and supervisory staff needs to be examined and implemented urgently. There is an urgent need to bring the administrative expenses to a figure of around 10%.

Reduction of surplus staff can be done by implementing VRS in respect of an estimated 100 officers, 500 regular staff, and 1100 other daily wage earners and casual workers. Unless the administrative expenditure is controlled by close monitoring and regular review, and new business is generated, the viability of MPHB is likely to be threatened seriously.

Voluntary Retirement Scheme

MPHB has assessed the number of staff who are likely to avail VRS and evolved an appropriate scheme. Around 1700 staff members, out of a total of 3823, are expected to avail the scheme. The estimated cost of its implementation is Rs. 24.40 crores. The break up of staff and the estimated cost as worked out by MPHB is given below in Table 5.3.

Table 5.3
Estimated of Cost of VRS

(Rs. in lakhs)

Period	*Officers*		*Other Staff (Regular)*		*WC, DW & CW*		*Total*	
	No	*Amount*	*No*	*Amount*	*No*	*Amount*	*No*	*Amount*
Upto 3/98	10	50.00	50	150.00	100	40.00	160	240.00
Upto 9/98	20	100.00	100	300.00	200	80.00	320	480.00
Upto 3/99	30	150.00	150	450.00	300	120.00	480	720.00
Upto 2000	40	200.00	200	600.00	500	200.00	740	1000.00
Total	100	500.00	500	1500.00	1100	440.00	1700	2440.00

WC - Work Charged, DW - Daily Wages, CW - Casual Workers

Notes: 1. Cost of VRS for an officer is Rs. 5.00 lakhs, for a staff member Rs. 3.00 lakhs, and for a WC person Rs. 0.4 lakh.

2. There will be a substantial increase in the cost of VRS if the pay revision recommendations are implemented. There may be an upward revision in daily wages and wages paid to casual workers also.

The scheme needs to be looked into carefully and designed properly to suit the needs of the Housing Board.

Cost of Construction

The Housing Board has developed its own norms for fixation, valuation, and transfer of assets under the provisions of the MP Housing Board Act and Rules. This may have to be reviewed in the light of the latest developments. The cost of construction of EWS and LIG housing comes to Rs. 160 - Rs. 230 per sft. For MIG and HIG housing, it ranges from Rs. 275 to Rs. 325 per sft. depending on specifications, design, etc. The cost of construction of MPHB compares favourably as it is on the lower side by 15% - 20% than that of the MP Police Housing Corporation (MPPHC) and PWD. This is probably due to the larger quantum of work, more experience and technical personnel in MPHB.

Supervision Charges

MPHB charges different rates of interest for different categories of houses. It also levies supervision charges as percentage of cost of construction as shown in Table 5.4.

Table 5.4

Category	*Rate of Interest*	*Supervision charges*
EWS	12%	7%
LIG	13.5%	9%
MIG	17%	17%
HIG	17%	17%

The supervision charges are levied at differential rates for different income groups — lower rates of 7% and 9% for economically weaker sections and low income groups respectively, and 12% for middle and higher income groups. These differential rates are prescribed perhaps with a social objective in view but not based on specific costs of construction since the financial viability of the Board finally rests on income left over after meeting all costs of construction, including administrative expenses. A system based on sound rationale, keeping in view the costs of construction, as well as the social objective, will have to be worked out while determining the differential rates of supervision charges. This needs to be properly reflected in pricing the developed plots and houses built so as to achieve the economies of scale. It is also necessary to plan for building a larger number of houses. These steps will not only improve the annual turnover, but also help establish a meaningful correlation between the Board's turnover and profitability.

Justification

At present housing activity is mostly in the private sector and is demand-driven in urban areas. Real estate activity has picked up considerably in important towns and commerical areas. A question arises whether the State should be involved in this activity or should withdraw, or at least roll back to some extent in this activity. It is in this context that we have to examine whether there is need for the continuance of MPHB. It has, however, to be kept in mind that the private sector, in spite of its efficiency, is not serving the weaker sections, nor facilitating the low and middle income group persons, to own a house. Moreover, the construction activity of the private sector at present is limited to cities only. On the other hand, MPHB is undertaking construction of houses for the low, middle and high income groups, not only in cities but also at District Headquarters and Growth Centres, by availing the facility of hire-purchase system of HUDCO. Another advantage of a Housing Scheme undertaken by the Housing Board is that it adheres to the norms stipulated by the Town Planning and Municipal authorities. It also provides for civic amenites which are at times neglected by the private sector. There is thus a good case for continuing its activity. Otherwise, the needy, low and middle income groups will be deprived of this basic facility of owning a house. Besides, the Housing Board is also undertaking infrastructural work for bridges, roads, preparation of master plans, etc., in consonance with Government policy. It is also instrumental in implementing the Housing Policy of the Madhya Pradesh Government by developing cheaper building components for economic house building and to develop skilled labour like masons, maistries, etc., by organizing training programmes to improve their skills, particularly concentrating on SC/ST candidates with a social objective.

The generally accepted test and touchstone for determining the need for a public sector presence is social purpose served, viability and profitability, availability of alternative means, ability to raise finances from the open market and whether it is competitive and efficient. MPHB is a statutory Board set up by Government to implement the policy of the Government and serves a socially relevant purpose. The questions that are not unequivocally answered are about demonstrated capacity to raise resources, deployment of such resources effectively and competitively, and ability to ensure continuous growth. MPHB scores in its objectives and social values but needs to improve its functioning and efficiency. It should rely more on its competence and less on Government or budgetary support, except where it can enable it to secure additional strengths or synergy.

Recommendations

MPHB has a reasonable component of professional expertise and technical know-how to formulate and execute the housing schemes in the State of Madhya Pradesh. It has promoted Awas Vikas Sansthan for creating a network of Building Centres in the State. So far 22 Building Centres of Awas Vikas Sansthan have been sanctioned by HUDCO. The Centres are imparting training to masons, plumbers, carpenters, etc., in the production and use of low-cost and cost-effective building material. The Board is able to take up infrastructure development like construction of bridges on rivers, major roads, etc. It has undertaken a number of major projects like developing Satellite Townships at Bhopal, Gwalior, Sagar, etc. The Board also organizes common services, maintenance of security, plantations, cleaning and scavenging, water supply, etc. It has carried out a number of deposit works, including World Bank Projects, Navodaya, and Tribal, SC, BC development works. More importantly, it has not defaulted in in loan repayments and receives favourable consideration from HUDCO in the matter of sourcing finance for its housing schemes. There is thus a case for its continuance but it has to reduce expenditure on staff, improve efficiency, cut costs and time of construction, secure more work orders, improve recoveries of dues, do a full-fledged costing exercise and re-position itself as an effective Housing Board.

It should be possible to prepare a Corporate Plan to enable MPHB to become a self-reliant organization that can raise capital and work profitably to serve the social cause. Greater professionalism and capacity building could help it in its tasks ahead.

The Housing Board has a good spread across the length and breadth of a sprawling State like Madhya Pradesh. It has a large contingent of manpower, including engineering and professional staff. It has the capacity and professional competence to handle more work. With better work culture and efficient functioning, it has scope to reduce its costs of operation by optimum utilization of its resources. It can attract funds from various financial institutions and the open market and further expand its areas of activity. It can take up bigger multi-storeyed buildings in urban areas and selective works in rural areas. Moreover, it is important to note that it has been working on profitable lines for more than a decade and enlargement of its activity can ensure economies of scale and reduce its costs of operation considerably.

Against this background, there is need to examine whether the related housing activity of the State, which is now being undertaken by several agencies of the State Government, can be brought under a single umbrella. MPHB has better professional expertise and technical know-how needed for construction activity and has extra unutilized capacity to undertake worth. It may perhaps be necessary to examine the need for an agency like MPPHC to undertake a relatively small quantum of work when MPHB or other agencies can more economically and effectively do this work. This will also result in economies of scale and reduction of expenditure for the State. MPHB has been operating without incurring losses, though not very profitably, while MPPHC has been incurring losses continuously, except for one year. Besides, the activity level of MPPHC is so low that it can perhaps be conveniently clubbed with MPHB. An exclusive Wing or Cell under the auspices of MPHB could easily undertake the present work of MPPHC and the State could benefit from the reduction of expenditure on MPPHC and economies of scale operations of MPHB. This will, however, need detailed examination.

Analysis of Steps for Merger of MPHB and MPPHC

MPHB was established under the Madhya Pradesh Griha Nirman Mandal Adhiniyam of 1972, whereas MPPHC was formed under the Companies Act of 1956. The merger of these two organizations will pose certain technical problems and legal hurdles. Keeping in view the legal and practical problems involved, and the highly time-consuming process, it is proposed that MPPHC be wound up voluntarily under Section 484(1) of the Companies Act. It would be a smoother and easy process which can be implemented quickly, surmounting the practical and legal hassles involved in a merger.

The activity of MPPHC can be carried out under a separate wing of MPHB, where no separate identity is needed for MPPHC, especially for the purpose of raising funds from various financial sources. MPHB can undertake execution of work of housing schemes on behalf of a local authority or Cooperative Housing Society or any other body, whether Government or otherwise, under Section 32 of the MP Griha Nirman Mandal Adhiniyam, 1972.

Under the above provision, the construction activity of MPPHC can be brought under the direct purview of MPHB, establishing a separate wing at MPHB Headquarters to monitor and supervise the execution of works hitherto undertaken by MPPHC.

When once the voluntary winding up of MPPHC is decided upon, the following steps are indicated broadly to wind up MPPHC and to take up its activities under the umbrella of MPHB:

- MPPHC should pass a Resolution that the company be wound up voluntarily. It is a Resolution passed under Clause (b) of Sub-section (1) of Section 484 of the Companies Act "for voluntary winding up".

- After passing the Resolution for voluntary winding up, it shall, within 14 days of the passing of the Resolution, give notice of the Resolution by advertisement in the Official Gazette and also in some newspapers circulating in the district where the Registered Office of the Company is situated.

- When it is proposed to wind up voluntarily, its Directors, or a majority of its Directors when there are more than two, may make a Declaration, verified by an Affidavit at a meeting of the Board, to the effect that they have made a full enquiry into the affairs of the company and that they have formed the opinion that the company has no debts, or that it will be able to pay its debts in full within such period, not exceeding three years from the commencement of winding up.

- Such a Declaration shall be made within five weeks immediately preceding the date of passing of the Resolution for winding up the company. It shall be accompanied by a copy of the Report of the Auditors of the Company on the Profit and Loss Account of the Company.

- The company in General Meeting shall appoint one or more Liquidators for the purpose of winding up the affairs and distributing the assets of the company. The company may fix the remuneration, if any, to be paid to the Liquidator(s).

- If the Liquidator is at any time of the opinion that the company will not be able to pay its debts in full within the period stated in the Declaration, or that period has expired without the debts having been paid in full, he shall forthwith summon a meeting of creditors, and shall lay before the meeting a Statement of Assets and Liabilities of the Company.

- As soon as the affairs of the company are fully wound up, the Liquidator shall make up an account of the winding up, showing how the winding up has been conducted and the property of the company has been disposed of. A General Meeting of the Company shall be called for the purpose of laying the account before it. This meeting shall be called by the advertisement, specifying the date, time, place and object of the meeting.
- So far as the employees of MPPHC are concerned, except for those whom MPPHC may like to retain, the others may be offered the benefits of VRS, since they cannot be absorbed into MPHB where there is a already proposal to extend VRS for 1700 employees who are found surplus.

Enclosures

Annexure I : Statement of Staff Strength

Annexure II : Histogram on Houses and Plots

Annexure III : Statement on Sources of Finance

Annexure IV : Statement on Important Financial Indicators

Annexure-I

Statement Showing Staff Strength of Madhya Pradesh Housing Board

Category	*Class I*	*Class II*	*Class III*	*Class IV*	*Casual Labour*	*Daily Wage Employees*	*Co-terminal Basis*		*Employees on Deputation*		*Employees on Muster Rolls*		*Raipur Jabalpur Bhilai*		*Total*
							III	*IV*	*III*	*IV*	*III*	*IV*	*III*	*IV*	
Technical	68	129	600	83	13	5	Nil	Nil	1	Nil	5	50	75	33	1066
Administrative	29	44	1210	640	141	17	4	4	3	Nil	27	526	79	33	2757
Total	97	173	1810	723	154	22	4	4	4	Nil	32	576	154	66	3823

Annexure-II

MP Housing Board

	1993-94	*1994-95*	*1995-96*	*1996-97*
House				
Target	5500	6000	6200	5700
Achievement	4831	4116	4167	3935
Plots				
Target	10000	11000	10500	11500
Achievement	8540	9135	6512	6750

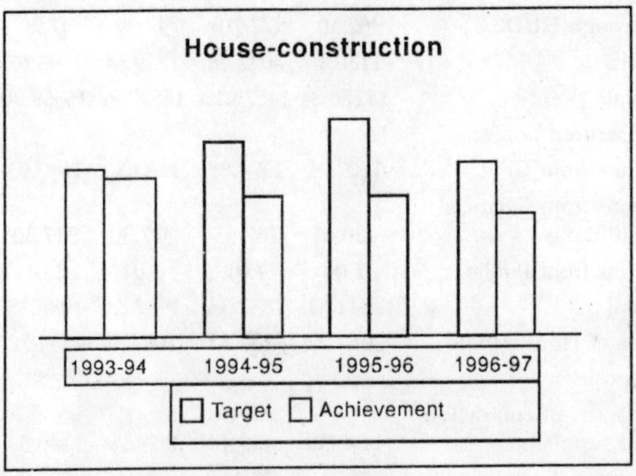

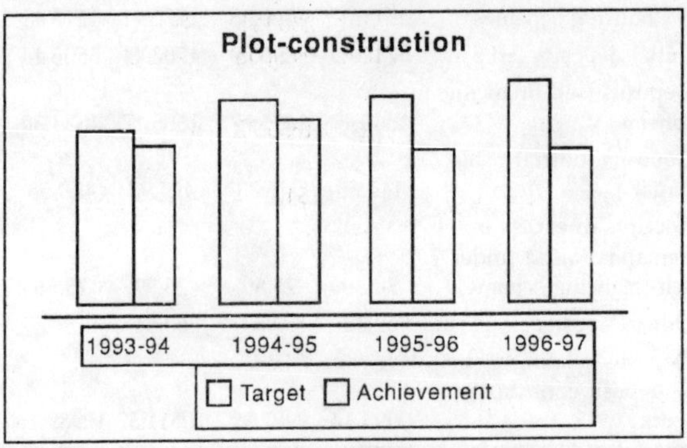

Annexure-III

Sources of Finance for MPHB

(Rs. in lakhs)

S. No.	*Details*	*1992-93*	*1993-94*	*1994-95*	*1995-96*	*1996-97*
A.	Secured Loans:					
1.	Debentures	3044.30	3305.30	3566.23	34524.73	3675.73
2.	Loans from banks	2.05	2.05	2.05	197.42	72.03
3.	Loans from MPHB (WBP)	97.71	99.12	(59.42)	(0.40)	-
4.	Loan from WBP Navodaya	-	-	60.50	92.07	-
5.	HUDCO DIC (direct)	3080.52	4713.39	6345.73	7058.79	8272.32
6.	LIC (through Govt)	1451.51	1541.63	1445.29	1329.32	2773.17
7.	GIC	438.34	421.04	408.24	389.81	1197.73
8.	Other institutions	1968.67	2540.84	2317.20	2426.95	3237.23
9.	World Bank (through HUDCO)	62.50	(72.70)	47.29	47.29	47.29
10.	NHB	1130.40	2022.46	1739.84	1593.87	1250.77
	Total	11276.04	14573.15	15892.99	16659.90	20526.32
B	Unsecured Loans:					
1.	Loans from Govt.	1602.32	1574.88	1665.50	1667.93	1667.76
2.	Loans from Financial Institutions	438.44	287.65	317.30	317.30	400.26
3.	Loans from Public	1.04	1.04	1.04	1.04	1.04
	Total	2041.81	1863.58	1983.84	1986.28	2069.07
C	Sale of House/Plots	2984.27	3132.33	10121.17	4384.72	2830.36
D.	Deposits:					
1.	Deposits of contractors and suppliers	1108.36	1199.40	1174.79	1190.56	1378.00
2.	Tenancy deposits	78.71	79.11	79.31	79.62	80.99
3.	Registration deposits for housing schemes	2511.02	2360.35	1472.91	1213.41	1417.61
4.	Initial deposits (HPS)	5712.69	7895.99	4702.44	5506.44	7490.64
5.	Deposits (self-financing scheme)	1660.49	1635.77	1605.17	1834.30	820.73
6.	Deposits (outright sale basis)	445.66	546.33	424.93	470.58	486.99
7.	Receipts in excess of demands raised under self-financing scheme	54.39	25.89	25.59	25.66	434.15
8.	Other deposits	52.35	59.53	60.64		
9.	Deposits relating to deposit contribution work	9995.14	9907.99	10511.57	10989.15	1359.87
	Total	20620.81	23710.36	20057.35	21309.72	25706.98

Annexure-IV

Important Financial Indicators of MPHB

S. No.	*Details*	*Figures from Balance Sheets*				
		1992-93	*1993-94*	*1994-95*	*1995-96*	*1996-97*
1.	Sale of Houses/plots	2984.27	3132.33	10121.17	4384.72	2830.36
2.	Cost of sales	3733.95	5794.57	10828.43	4676.75	2895.86
3.	Gross profit	155.41	264.36	530.70	464.07	362.05
4.	Depreciation	19.83	20.05	19.74	19.65	27.64
5.	Overhead interests	569.22	293.09	1479.02	1523.59	2411.87
6.	Net profit	142.09	55.86	151.63	81.37	70.08
7.	Gross profit margin (%) (3 divided by 1)	5.21	8.44	5.24	10.58	12.79
8.	Net profit margin (%) (6 divided by 1)	4.76	1.78	1.50	1.86	2.48
9.	Capital (factory)	402.25	712.80	758.15	784.41	800.02
10.	Reserves & surplus (capital reserve)	3592.81	4603.58	5187.86	6183.76	6550.75
11.	Fixed assets	909.97	940.03	1314.28	1395.57	1449.42
12.	Investments	1504.26	2829.32	3113.02	4270.02	4724.85
13.	Current assets	48050.46	54643.12	54165.58	61111.04	65339.84
14.	Current Liabilities	33148.18	36659.35	34790.04	41162.28	41567.95
15.	Current ratio	1.45	1.49	1.56	1.48	1.57

7

Madhya Pradesh Police Housing Corporation

Introduction

The Madhya Pradesh Police Housing Corporation (MPPHC) was incorporated in the year 1971 as a Private Limited Company under the Companies Act, 1956, with the main purpose of building houses for police personnel working in various parts of the State of Madhya Pradesh. The service conditions of police personnel provide for rent-free living accommodation. There is, however a wide gap between the available government accommodation and number of police personnel. MPPHC is expected to bridge the gap by constructing new houses for the Police Department.

Objectives

The main objectives of the Corporation are:

- To formulate and execute housing schemes for the benefit of serving employees of the Government of Madhya Pradesh in the Police Department;
- To undertake construction of office and residential buildings and provision of common facilities like community hall, hospital, water tank, electricity, sanitary facilities or other conveniences, for housing police employees of the Government of Madhya

Pradesh, either directly or through contractors or other agency; and

- To purchase and sell houses and buildings.

Need for Police Housing

Policemen are subjected to rough and tough working conditions, based in remote corners of the State, and under stress as they have to attend to duties round the clock. Suitable provision of housing will boost their morale. Government wish to provide a better degree of employee housing satisfaction and indirectly improve the efficiency of police personnel. Hence, MPPHC was set up.

Need for a State Organization

The National Housing Policy envisages the role of housing agencies as one of facilitators and promoters of housing and urban development. The National as well as the State-level Housing Policies perceive the Government's new role as that of an "Enabler" rather than as a "Provider" of all resources and services. In the changed scenario, there may be no need for the Government to undertake construction and building activity by itself if the job can be got done through other agencies. The same activity can be easily carried out through private contractors at lower costs, with Government undertaking only the monitoring function. However, when a separate organization is created, it should fulfil the objectives in an efficient, cost effective and competitive manner.

Organizational Structure

The Registered Office of MPPHC is at Bhopal. Five Divisional Offices are located at Bhopal, Indore, Gwalior, Jabalpur and Raipur. The Board of 12 Directors, and a Chief Executive designated as Managing Director, are all nominated by the Government. The Board is responsible for direction, superintendence, control and guidance of the Corporation. The Board meets at least once in a quarter to transact business. The Board has nominees from Government Departments or public sector undertakings engaged in similar nature of activities. They represent the Public Works Department (PWD), Town and Country Planning, Electricity Board, Housing & Urban Development Corporation, etc. There is no fixed tenure of office. As the Directors are Government Officials, there are frequent changes in the Board due to the postings of these officers.

Personnel

The total number of staff working in the corporation is 241, including 14 members drawn on deputation from other departments, against the sanctioned strength of 278.

Table 7.1
Personnel Position

S. No.	*Description*	*Engg.*	*Ministerial Staff*	*Class IV*	*Total*
1.	No. of persons in position	73	94	60	227
2.	No. of officers on deputation from other Departments to MPPHC	8	6	-	14
3.	Total	81	100	60	241

Capital Structure

The capital structure of an enterprise comprises long term debt and equity. The relationship between such long term debt and equity is termed as the debt equity ratio. The capital structure of an enterprise should be so designed as to maximize the earnings per share without commensurately increasing the risk. The debt equity ratio in 1992-93 was 12:1 for MPPHC. It shot up to 26:1 in 1995-96. The debt equity ratio declined to 10:1 in 1996-97 due to the infusion of equity of Rs. 400 lakhs. It could be surmised that the capital structure of the corporation did not suit its financial requirements as MPPHC incurred cash losses between 1992-93 and 1996-97, except for the year 1995-96.

Funding of MPPHC

MPPHC is funded through interest free loan made available by the Government to provide for the seed money and to repay loans obtained from financial institutions by MPPHC.

MPPHC uses the Government funds as seed money to raise funds from financial institutions to build houses and hand them over to Government. 30% of the loan is used as seed money and 70% loan is obtained from financial institutions. After the Government accepts the buildings, it accepts the liability to pay the instalments of principal and loan of financial institutions. MPPHC is thus used as an agency to source extra budgetary funds.

After the houses are constructed, the cost is fixed and the assets transferred to Government. The value of assets transferred is adjusted against the amount of interest free loan sanctioned by Government. MPPHC is paid 10% of the cost of construction as service charge to cover its expenses.

External Loans

MPPHC raised funds from various financial institutions as detailed below:

Table 7.2
Sources of External Loans

(Rs. in Lakhs)

S. No.	*Source*	*1994-95*	*1995-96*	*1996-97*
1.	HUDCO	129.18	947.26	942.06
2.	State Bank of Indore	400.00	454.14	-
3.	Indian Overseas Bank	-	100.00	-
4.	Total	529.18	1501.40	942.06

The repayment term of loans varies from 4 to 8 years. Repayments are made quarterly from interest free loan received from the Government.

Construction Activity

The number of houses built vis-a-vis the targets fixed for the last fours are indicated below:

Table 7.3
Houses Constructed

S. No.	*Source*	*1994-95*	*1995-96*	*1996-97*
1.	1994-95	924	937	100%
2.	1995-96	1448	1259	87%
3.	1996-97	1308	573	44% 78.33
4.	1997-98	1254 2562	1434 2007	114% %
5.	Total	4934	4203	85%

It is noted that there are uneven levels of performance. According to MPPHC, the main reason for shortfall in targets is the failure on the part of Government to provide adequate funds in time. Money is often released towards the fag end of the financial year, resulting in delayed/inadequate payments to the contractors who do not fulfil their commitments.

The Government/Police Department fix the targets of houses to be constructed for police personnel every year and provide appropriate budgetary support. The target of MPPHC is to construct 1500 houses per year. MPPHC has reported that the pace of construction has been affected due to inadequate budgetary support and delays in release of funds, apart from detailed Government scrutiny for sanction. According to MPPHC, as a result the progress of work is not commensurate with their capacity and hence only 57% of the target has been achieved. As the main objective of MPPHC is to expedite police housing, it should have put in adequate effort in pursuing with the agencies of Government to release adequate funds in time to match the targets of construction fixed each year. It appears open market by way of Bonds, etc., to supplement Government funds releases. MPPHC appears to have taken a passive role and not that of a pro-active housing development company.

Cost of Construction

The cost of construction per sft by MPPHC vis-a-vis PWD is furnished below region-wise:

Table 7.4
Comparative Cost of Construction

S. No.	*Region*	*PWD*	*MPPHC*
		Cost per sft (in Rs.)	
1.	Indore	291	302
2.	Bhopal	262	272
3.	Raipur	240	312
4.	Gwalior	308	318

The cost of construction by MPPHC is higher than that of the State PWD.

Administrative Expenses

Administrative expenses have increased from Rs. 13 lakhs during 1992-93 to Rs. 21.80 lakhs in 1995-96. They were Rs. 18.83 lakhs in 1996-97. However, there has been no significant increase in the level of construction activity. Against the fee paid by Government of 10% of turnover as supervision charges, the administrative expenses have been higher and in the range of 12 to 20%. MPPHC needs to tighten its belt and reduce the cost of construction by downsizing its staff, enhancing its construction activity, farming out work, and by utilizing local building materials. There is an urgent need to contain the administrative expenses by reducing the redundant staff, if necessary by resorting to a voluntary retirement scheme (VRS).

Income

According to MPPHC, the quantum of work entrusted and executed so far has been lower than the capacity, reportedly due to dearth of funds which do not provide the level and tempo of activity required to be taken up in order to break-even. The corporation should operate with minimum core staff, farm out work, and maximize turnover of Government, and supplement it with works of other clients as well if there is square capacity. The ability to secure finances in time, plan properly and maximize turnover while operating economically holds the key to success. The corporation appears to have adopted a laid back attitude and not been active enough to secure funds from Government and other sources in time, improve efficiency, cut staff costs, reduce cost of construction and develop competence and credibility to raise funds from the open market.

Profit and Loss

The MPPHC has been incuring losses for the last five years, except in 1995-96. The main reason for the losses is the low annual turnover as detailed below:

Table 7.5
Turnover and Profit and Loss

(Rs. in Lakhs)

Year	*Annual Turnover*	*Profit or Loss*
1992-93	619.81	-40.72
1993-94	795.04	-41.52
1994-95	1010.26	-38.44
1995-96	1754.94	30.89
1996-97	1451.40	-26.35

It is difficult for the corporation to break-even unless the annual turnover is at least Rs. 1700 lakhs.

Overall Financial Performance

MPPHC's total revenue has more than doubled between 1992-93 and 1996-97, but the corporation could earn marginal profits only in 1995-96. As revealed by the data provided hereunder, the major portion of revenue was utilized for paying salaries and wages.

Table 7.6
Proportion of Salaries and Wages to Total Revenue and Total Cost

Percentage of Salaries and wages to:	*1992-93*	*1993-94*	*1994-95*	*1995-96*	*1996-97*
- Total Revenue	91.39	77.96	76.79	56.00	82.60
- Total Cost	57.60	53.01	57.81	69.90	72.26

The growing share of salaries and wages in total operation cost has adversely affected the bottom line of the corporation.

The losses of the corporation would have been much higher if interest was paid on the loans. During the period under reference, no interest has been paid/accounted for on the loans received by the corporation.

The corporation suffered from a surfeit of working capital. Receivables constituted the major portion of the corporation's total current assets. It appears that a significant portion of investments in receivables had fallen overdue for a long period.

A prompt recovery of such dues would make the corporation financially sound. The corporation's net worth turned negative in 1993-94. Due to infusion of fresh equity by the State Government, its net worth could become positive at the end of 1996-97.

The financial performance of the corporation has remained dismal. This is seen from the fact that the gross margin for the corporation was always negative, save in 1995-

96. This was due both to high operating costs incurred by MPPHC and its lack of success to boost its revenue to the required extent. The operating loss as a percentage of capital employed shot up from 1.82% in 1992-93 to 4.29% in 1996-97.

The salient data about the financial performance of the corporation are given in Table 7.7.

Table 7.7
Major Financial Aggregates

(Rs. in Lakhs)

Sl. No.	*Head*	*1992-93*	*1993-94*	*1994-95*	*1995-96*	*1996-97*
1.	Equity capital	200.00	200.00	200.00	200.00	600.00
2.	Loans from Government, banks & financial institutions	2377.78	3457.69	3710.28	5243.36	6036.33
3.	Working capital	2393.80	3411.63	3600.48	5155.18	6322.76
4.	Total capital employed	2409.08	3446.17	3659.47	5225.91	6390.94
5.	Net worth	31.30	-11.52	-50.81	-17.45	354.60
6.	Total revenue	63.87	80.21	103.09	188.07	150.84
7.	Salaries, wages and allowances	58.37	62.53	79.16	105.28	124.60
8.	Administrative expenses	13.00	14.29	18.54	21.80	18.83
9.	Others	27.84	37.47	35.78	20.60	24.80
10.	Cost of operation	101.34	117.95	136.92	150.61	170.07
11.	Gross margin	-37.47	-71.57	-33.83	37.46	-19.23
12.	Depreciation	3.26	3.78	4.61	6.56	7.12
13.	Profit	-40.72	-41.52	-38.44	30.89	-26.35
14.	Cash losses (accumulated losses)	168.70	211.92	250.81	217.45	244.07
15.	Operating loss as a percentage of capital employed.	-1.82%	-1.26%	-1.13%	0.62%	-4.29%

Should MPPHC be Retained?

The following aspects need serious attention regarding the utility and continuance of a separate MPPHC:

- The MPPHC is not professionally well equipped to take up house construction work. They draw engineers on deputation from Government's PWD to take up construction work under its supervision. The MP Housing Board (MPHB), another Government agency with a State-wide spread, has its own cadre of engineers and professional expertise to take up house construction. There is avoidable overlap of functions.
- Its achievement against target is only around 57%. This is reportedly due to lack of adequate budgetary support from Government and paucity of funds.
- It has not been able to contain costs within the supervisory charges fixed Government, indicating poor levels of efficiency, low turnover and high level of staff. Productivity does not appear to be satisfactory.
- The cost of construction is relatively higher than that of PWD and MPHB.
- MPPHC draws 30% of the seed money from Government and balance 70% from other agencies and financial institutions. It has played a very passive role and has not been able to raise funds from the market to serve its objectives.
- It has not been able to supplement its income and reduce its costs of operation.
- It has incurred net losses all through except in 1995-96, and eroded its net worth completely by 1993-94. However, due to an infusion of Rs. 400 lakhs towards equity in 1996-97, the net worth again became positive during the penultimate year of the study.
- It appears that the professional, financial and technical, and supervisory inputs have not been adequate to achieve the objectives for which the corporation was set up.

Under these circumstances, it is rather difficult for this organization to turnaround and make profits.

It needs serious consideration whether its work can be entrusted to the Housing Board which, with its larger spread, better know-how, and technical expertise, could be a better course of action.

Recommendation

Against this background, it has to be examined whether it is desirable and economical to continue MPPHC as a separate entity, or whether its activities can be clubbed with another organization. It is well nigh impossible for MPPHC to break-even unless its turnover is substantially improved and the administrative expenses are brought below 10% of its turnover which is the level of its income. Presently, with an annual turnover widely fluctuating much below Rs. 1700 lakhs, it is considered neither feasible nor economical to continue MPPHC, particularly in view of the fact that administrative overheads would far outweigh the activity level, thus vitiating the very objective for which the corporation was formed.

However, MPPHC was formed with the specific purpose of catering to the housing needs of the police personnel in the State. This may be well served with an exclusive cell for the housing requirements of police personnel attached to the MP Housing Board, which can take care of the housing activity of the State under a single umbrella. It will also ensure better quality of work as police personnel can refuse to accept houses of poor quality which would otherwise be difficult when it is placed under the supervision of their own senior officers. Since the objective of both the organizations are more or less similar, if not identical, clubbing them under one organization with a separate wing for Police Housing would be economical and desirable. Pending a final decision on this issue, VRS may be implemented in MPPHC to prune the excess staff and reduce losses in this organization.

Select Bibliography

Abani, AS, Cost Audit and Public Enterprises with Special Reference to Rajasthan, *Lok Udyog,* 7(2), 1973. pp 35-39.

Budgeting in Public Enterprises: A Case Study of Rajasthan Government Enterprises, *Lok Udyog,* 7(12), 1974, pp. 49-57.

Professional Management in State Level Public Enterprises, *Lok Udyog,* 11(12), 1978 pp. 29-34.

Adiseshiah, Malcolms, Privatisation and State Enterprises, Calcutta, IIM, 1989, 48p.

Agarwal, RC, *State Enterprise in India,* Allahabad, Chaitanya Publishing House, 1961, 271p.

ALAM, M, BSAIDC's (Bihar State Agro Industries Development Corporation) Help to Farmers. *Economic Times,* 4 December, 1977, p. 10.

Amin, GD, GIIC (Gujarat Industrial Investment Corporation) Serves Social Contact of Plannning, *Eastern Economist,* 7 December, 1973, pp. 1058-1059.

Andhra Pradesh Public Enterprise Management Board, Andhra Pradesh State Public Enterprises Performance during 1986-87. Public Enterprise Management Board, Hyderabad, 1987.

Appa Rao, B, *Small Enterprise Promotion in Andhra Pradesh*: Role of Andhra Pradesh State Financial Corporation, 1981, 23p.

Arumugam, K, BSCIC (Bihar State Credit and Investment Corporation) Boon to Private Sector. *Economic Times,* 4 December, 1977, p. 3.

Asthana, P, Role of Uttar Pradesh Financial Corporation *Eastern Economist,* 21 January, 1972, pp. 89-95.

Atmanand, Bihar's Public Enterprises: Constraints and Options. *Economic Times,* October 24, 1989, p. 7.

Aziz, A, Management Problems of State Public Undertakings. Jaipur, Printwell, 1990.

Bajuleyan, KS, Achievements of Kerala Urban Development Finance Corporation, Quarterly Journal of the Local Self Government Institute, 47(2), 1976. pp. 208-215.

Bakkappa, B, Karnataka Public Sector Enterprises Need a Policy and Preferential Enterprise, *Southern Economist,* 25(13), 1986, pp. 17-19.

Bakshi, PM, State Enterprises and Arbitration, *Financial Express,* April 24, 1989.

Bansal, S and Agarwal, VK, Social Responsibility of State Entreprise, *Yojana,* 30(17), September 16-39, 1986, pp. 20-25.

Basu, SC, West Bengal Financial Corporation, *Yojana,* 29 November, 1970. p. 41.

Basu, SK, Sarkar, A and Sinha, HN, Report on the Monetary and Non-Monetary Work Incentives in Public Enterprises of West Bengal, Book Exchange, Calcutta 1971, xxxii; 111p.

Batra, GS, Legislative and Executive Control of Public Enterprises of Punjab (Abstract of Thesis). Indian Journal of Public Enterprise, June 1993, pp. 111-115.

Batra, GS and Bhatia, BS, Top Management Structure and Accountability for Public Enterprises (A Case Study of Punjab) *NMIMS Management Review,* January-June, 1994, pp. 83-102.

Batra, Satish K, Admissibility of Questions on State Enterprises of Rajasthan Legisltive Assembly: Some Issues, *Administrative Change*, 3(1), 1975, pp. 97-108.

Batra, Satish and Jain, Tej K (Eds.) *State Enterprises: The Emerging Scenario*, Jaipur, Printwell Publishers, 1988, 2 Vols.

Bhambhri, CP, *Parliamentary Control over State Enterprises in India*, Delhi, Metropolitan Book Co., 1960, 115p.

Bhandari, KC, *Nationalisation of Industries in India.* Calcutta, Academic Press, 1962, xi; 221p.

Bhanu Prasad Committee, Management of State Level Public Enterprises: *Report.* n.p. 1987, 16p.

Bhardwaj, HC, New Lease of Life for HP. *Sunday Observer*, August 21, 1994, p. VIII.

Bhargava, PK, Public Enterprises in Uttar Pradesh. *Indian Journal of Commerce*, 21(4) December 1968, pp. 100-108.

Bhat, KS and Nandagopal, R, Role of Chairmen and Managing Directors in State Level Public Enterprises: A Discussion. Hyderabad, *Institute of Public Enterprise*, 1991. 8p.

Bhat, SA, Management of Public Enterprises, Delhi, Anmol Publications, 1991. 120p.

Chari, VV, Performance Problems of State Financial Corporations, *Commerce*, December, 1974. pp. 173-180.

Chatha, AS, PSIDC (Punjab State Industrial Development Corporation) Forges Ahead. *Eastern Economist*, 8 November, 1974. pp. 31-33.

Chatterjee, Bibhas, West Bengal: How to Life the State Undertakings from the Morass. *Capital*, 14 April, 1977, pp. 485-486.

Chattopadhyay, P., Revamping the West Bengal Financial Corporation, *Capital,* 28 August, 1975. pp. 281-282.

Chauhan, Organisation and Working of Public Enterprises in Gujarat, Vallabh Vidyanagar, Sardar Patel University, 1978, viii; 580p.

Chinta Rao, N, Working Capital Management: A Study of Selected State Enterprises of Karnataka. Nagarjunanagar, Nagarjuna University, 1988. 412p.

Choyal, BR, Financial Management of State Enterprises, Jaipur, Printwell, 1986.

Dasgupta, BR, West Bengal Industrial Development Corporation and Industrial Development of West Bengal. India in Industries, 10(3), 1972. pp. 121-123.

Das Mahapatra, SN, Industrial Development Corporation of Orissa, *Lok Udyog,* 6(2) 1972, pp. 57-58, 66.

Dave, GL, Financial Management in Public Enterprises of Rajasthan State. *Institute of Public Enterprise Journal,* 11(4), 1988, pp. 41-46.

Desai, KV, MIDC's (Maharashtra Industrial Development Corporation), Activities in Pimpri Industrial Area *Commerce,* June 23, 1973, pp. 9-11.

Deshpande, Charudatta, SICOM will be the First State Corporation to be Privatised. *Economic Times,* September 14, 1994, p. 1.

Dhankar, BL, Public Enterprises in Rajasthan, *Economic Studies,* May-June 15(11-12), 1975. pp. 509-518.

Dhar, TN, Role and Responsibility of State Enterprises, *Indian Management,* June 18(6), 1979, pp. 2-5.

Diwakar Rao, PL (Ed.), Public Sector in Andhra Pradesh: A Handloom and Directory (With Special Supplement on Central Sector), Secunderabad, Utility Publication, 1988. 339p.

Doraiswamy, PK, Research on Public Enterprise Management: A Manager's Viewpoint. *Institute of Public Enterprise Journal,* July-September, 1982, p. 33.

Dube, Ramakrishna, State Financial Corporation in India University of Indore Research Journal, 2(1), 1973, pp. 51-62.

Dubey, Sanjeev, Financial Control and Management of Madhya Pradesh Export Corporation, *Indian Journal of Public Enterprise,* 8(15), December 1993. pp. 78-87.

Dutt, RC, State Enterprises in a Developing Country: The Indian Experience, 1950-1990. Delhi, Abhinav Publishers, 1990. 201p.

Economic Times, Destination Orissa. *Economic Times,* May 10, 1992, pp. 16-21.

Centre Clears Orissa's Three Aluminium Plants. *Economic Times,* May 27, 1992, pp. 13.

Government Willing to Disinvest upto 100 pc Stakes in Viable Sick PSUs. *Economic Times,* July 6, 1992. p. 4.

State May Disinvest PSU, *Economic Times,* November 19, 1992. p. 5.

Fernandez, Clarence and Ranade, Sanjay, State-run Companies Incur Rs. 3 crore Loss — Management of all Kinds: CAG. *Times of India,* July 18, 1992. p. 15.

Gandhi, GN, Pricing the Managers in State Enterprises, *Indian Management,* December 8(9), 1969. pp. 9-11, 17.

Gangadharam Pillai, V, Public Sector in Kerala. Trivandrum, Kerala Academy of Political Science, 1980. 235p.

Garg, Pawan Kumar, Financial Management of State Industrial Enterprises in Haryana, Kurukshetra University, 1991, 229p.

Gavini, Augustine L, Ancillaries of Public Enterprises in Andhra Pradesh: A Study in Structure, Growth and Performance. (Thesis submitted to the Osmania University). Hyderabad, 1990. 384p.

Geeta Gouri, State Level Public Enterprises (SLPEs). *Institute of Public Enterprise Journal,* July-September, 1982, p. 92.

Ghuman, BS, Public Enterprises — The Punjab Experience, *Economic Times,* June 1, 1990.

Gopalaswami, TV, Returns from State Enterprises. *Financial Express,* July 31 & August 1, 1992, p. 8.

Gouri Shankar Rao, P, State Level Public Enterprises of Kerala: A Case Study of the Problems of Financial Management. (Thesis submitted to Osmainia University). Hyderabad, 1989, 437p.

Govindarajan, SR, Development and Performance of State Level Public Enterprises in Andhra Pradesh, *Institute of Public Enterprise Journal,* 11(1). January-March 1988, pp. 1-23.

Gupta, Santosh Kumar, Financial Analysis of State Enterprise in Rajasthan, Jaipur, Rajasthan, 1990.

Gupta, Sunil Kumar, Accounting for Inflation in Public Sector of India with Special Reference to Himachal Pradesh State Corporations, Shimla, Himachal Pradesh University.

Guptha, GC, Role of Andhra Pradesh Enterprises Management Board — A Critical Appraisal. Hyderabad, *Institute of Public Enterprise,* 1986. 110p.

Haririan, Mehdi, State Owned Enterprise in a Mixed Economy. London, Westview Press, 1989, xv; 198p.

Hassan, Shabir, Public Enterprises in Economic Development. Delhi, Anmol Publications, 1987, xiii; 230p.

Hemlata Rao, Financial Performance of Public Enterprises. Jaipur, Printwell Publishers, 1987, viii; 182p.

Hooja, B, Committee on Public Undertakings and Recommendations Regarding the Better Management of State Enterprises, *Prashasnika,* 3(1), 1974, pp. 1-18.

State Sector Industries: Future Prospects. *Financial Express,* March 31, 1968, p. 12.

Hooja, Bhupendra, Some Problems of Management in the State Sector. *Prasnashika,* April-June 4(2), 1975, pp. 1-6.

State Enterprises in Rajasthan, *Rajasthan University News,* 2(1) March 1969, pp. 18-24.

Hoon, VN, Role of Financial Adviser in State Enterprises, *Capital,* December 20, 1962, pp. 916-19.

India. Comptroller and Auditor General Report, Government of Himachal Pradesh (No. 3), Commercial. Chandigarh, Controller, Printing and Stationery (UT), 1988, 119p.

State Government Public Enterprises - Concepts, Performance and Accountability. New Delhi, Indian Audit and Accounts Department, 1989. v; 220p.

India. Ministry of Home Affairs, Department of Personnel and Administrative Reforms, Report of the Standing Group of Management of Public Enterprises in the States. (Chairman: H K L Capoor). New Delhi, Lok Sabha Secretariat, 1964.

India, *Planning Commission,* Report of the Efficient Conduct of State Enterprises by Gorwala, AD, New Delhi, 1951, 18p.

Indian Institute of Public Administration, Administrative Problems of State Enterprises in India: Report of a Seminar, December 1957. New Delhi, IIPA, 1957. xiv; 188p.

Institute of Public Enterprise, Management of State Level Public Enterprises and its Privatisation. Hyderabad, Institute of Public Enterprise, 1993.

National Seminar on PE Reforms and Privatisation in State Level Public Enterprises - Strategies and Techniques. *Institute of Public Enterprise Journal,* 15(4), December, 1992, pp. 305-324.

Jain, Bimal, Personnel Administration and Industrial Democracy in Growing State Enterprises: A Case Study of Bhilai Steel Plant. *Indian Journal of Labour Economics,* 9(2-3), 1996. pp. 293-317.

Jain, RK, Capital Formation in State Enterprises in India: Comments by HK Paranjape and Prasad. *Indian Journal of Public Administration,* 7(1) 1961. pp. 57-91.

Jain, Ravi K, Working Capital Management of State Enterprises in India. Jaipur, National Publishing House, 1988, xii; 338p.

James, Biji, Performance Appraisal of State Owned Enterprises in Kerala. Agra, Agra University, 1989.

Jessica, Mary V, Performance of SFCs: A Study of APSFC and KSFC. (Submitted to Osmaina University). Hyderabad, Osmania University, 1993.

Jhabvala, Firdaus, Model of Motivation in State Enterprises in Underdeveloped Economies, *Indian Economic Review,* October 8(2), 1973. pp. 172-85.

Juran, MS, Garg, PK and Bodla, BS, Measuring Changes in Financial Health - A Study of Selected State Enterprises. *Institute of Public Enterprise Journal,* 13(4), 1990. pp. 348-360.

Kapur, SL, Development and Performance of State Level Enterprises in Punjab, *Institute of Public Enterprise Journal,* 11(2), 1988. pp. 77-106.

Kar, NC, Study of the Industrial Development Corporation of Orissa Ltd. as a State Enterprise. *Institute of Public Enterprise Journal*, 9(1), 1986. pp. 48-54.

Kar, NC, Mishra, RK and Shukla, MB, Public Sector in Bihar Analysis. *Financial Express*, November 21/22, 1988.

Khan, A and Arora, RK, Public Enterprise in India: A Study of the State Government Undertakings. New Delhi. Associated Publishers, 1975.

Khan, Tariq Ahmad, Budgeting Control in Jammu and Kashmir State Level Public Enterprises. Management Accountant, June 1991, pp. 426-427.

Khan, Zahid, Management of Working Capital in Public Sector Units: A Study of UP Government Undertakings. Bareilly, Rohilkhand University, 1983.

Kiran Kumar, RK, Cash Management in Selected State Level Manufacturing Public Enterprises in Andhra Pradesh (Submitted to Osmania University). Hyderabad, Osmania University, 1990, 478p.

Kolelkar, BD, Human Resources Development: A Study of Selected Public Sector Undertakings in Maharashtra and Goa. New Delhi, Northern Book Centre, 1993, xi; 169p.

Kotia, DK, Improving Working of State Financial Corporations and Commercial Banks. *Eastern Economist*, 19 November, 1976. pp. 1002-1006.

Krishnamachary, P, Readings in Public Enterprise: Investment Management in Public Enterprises, Jaipur, Printwell Publishers, 1990. 236p.

Krishnamurthy, Gopal, Corporate Taxation and Public Enterprises in State Sector. *Indian Journal of Commerce*, 26(2) 1973. pp. 565-71.

Krishnamurthy, HV, In Search of Experience - A Personal

Experience. P.U. Management Review, 8(1&2), January-December, 1985. pp. 45-52.

Kulkarni, GR and Rangarajan, C, State Sector and the Indian Economy. State Enterprise, January-March, 1982, pp. 1-16.

Kumar, A, Industrial Relations in Public Sector Undertakings in Orissa. *Indian Journal of Labour Economics,* October 19(3-4), 1977. pp. 65-72.

Kumar, Indra and James, Biji, Public Sector Enterprises in India. New Delhi, Commonwealth Publishers, ix; 183p.

Kusuma, N, Management Control System in Public Enterprises (Readings in Public Enterprises - I). Jaipur, Printwell Publications, 1990, 229p.

Lakshmana Rao, V, Economic Development of Andhra Pradesh. Delhi, B.R. Publishing Corporation, 1985. 158p.

Lakshmanan, UN, Role of Karnataka State Financial Corporation in Industrial Development of the State, *Mysore Economic Review,* 60(7), 1975. pp. 11-13.

Lionel, M, Dismal Performance by Andhra Pradesh Public Sector, *Economic Times,* April 6, 1994, p. 13.

Maharashtra State Bureau of Public Enterprises, Performance of State Public Enterprises, 1991-92. Bombay, Government Press, 1992, 248p.

Mahmood, AAH and Egstad, SO, Determinants of Public Enterprises Performance Finance and Development, 24(4), 1987, pp. 26-29.

Malladi, RP, Public Enterprises Performance Evaluation Criteria for Andhra Pradesh State Enterprises. Hyderabad, *Institute of Public Enterprise,* 1990, 56p.

Mallikarjanayya, G, Organisation and Working of Andhra

Pradesh State Financial Corporation, *Lok Udyog,* 8(6), 1974, pp. 55-59.

Mallikarjuna Rao, C, Andhra Pradesh Industrial Technical Consultancy Organisation -- A Case Study, *Journal of Institute of Public Enterprise,* 16(3&4), September & December 1993, pp. 143-151.

Malyarov, OV, State Sector in Independent India. State Enterprises, 3(4), 1984. pp. 312-321.

Mathur, DC, Wages in the Public Sector: A Study of Rajasthan State Enterprises, New Delhi, Mittal, 1990, 121p.

Mathur, Hari Mohan, Exploring Industrial Potential of Backward Regions: Greater Role of SFCs. *Industrial Times,* August 7, 1972, pp. 11-12.

Mathur, NS, Uttar Pradesh Financial Corporation, *Commerce,* June 24, 1972, pp. 49-50.

Mathur, VBL, Marketing Management in State Enterprises, *Prashasnika,* 1(3), 1972, pp. 57-63.

Mehta, GL, Public Sector Undertakings in Rajasthan, Socialist Congressman, August 15, 1969, pp. 46-48.

Mishra, RK, Financial Restructuring of State Level Public Enterprises. *Journal of Institute of Public Enterprise,* 17(3&4), 1994, pp. 110-116.

Mishra, RK and Nandagopal, R, Management of State Level Public Enterprises in Rajasthan. *Institute of Public Enterprise Journal,* Vol. XI, No. 1, 1988. pp. 64-77.

Mishra, RK, Nandagopal, R, and Suri Babu, P, Study Report on Financial Contribution and Requirements of State Level Public Enterprises in India. 2 Vols. Hyderabad, *Institute of Public Enterprise,* 1993.

Mishra, RK and Pakki Reddy, G, State Level Public Enterprises of Andhra Pradesh: Some Policy Perspectives. Decision, April-June, 1993. pp. 65-90.

Technical Note on the State Level Public Enterprises in AP. *Institute of Public Enterprise Journal,* 12(12), March, 1989, pp. 1-36.

Mishra, RK, Rattan Reddy, B and Mallikarjuna Rao, C, Working of State Level Public Enterprises in Andhra Pradesh: A Critical Evaluation. *Indian Journal of Public Enterprise,* 8(15), December 1993. pp. 68-73.

Mishra, RK, Ravishankar, S and Nandagopal, R (Eds), Management of State Level Public Enterprises in India, New Delhi, National Publishing House, 1989, xxix; 603p.

Mohan Rao, P, Andhra Pradesh State Police Housing Corporation Limited - A Perspective. *Indian Journal of Public Enterprise,* 9(16), June 1994. pp. 66-72.

Muniramappa, CM, Inventory Control in State Enterprises. *Eastern Economist,* September 5, 1969. pp. 436-439.

Naidu, Hanumantha Rao and Shankaraiah, A, Incidence of Accidents — A Study of the Singareni Collieries Co. Ltd. Journal of Institute of Public Enterprise, 16(3&4), September & December 1993. pp. 161-172.

Nandagopal, R, Board of Directors in State Level Public Enterprises. *Institute of Public Enterprise Journal,* 12(1), March 1989. pp. 37-47.

Nandagopal, R. Mishra, RK and Mohan, VK, Budgeting in State Level Public Enterprises of Andhra Pradesh and Tamil Nadu. Hyderabad, Institute of Public Enterprise, 1992, p. 191.

Narayanan, R, Performance and Development of State Level Enterprises of Kerala. Institute Public Enterprise Journal, 9(1) 1988. pp. 57-63.

National Productivity Council, NPC Agricultural Productivity Sector — Productivity Performance of State Steel Corporations, *Productivity,* January-March, 1989, pp. 493-494.

Nigam, Raj K, State Government Undertakings. *Commerce,* 22 June 1968 (Suppl.) p. 62-64.

Nunnenkanp, P, State Enterprises in Developing Countries. *Inter Economics,* 21(4), 1986, pp. 186-193.

Panda J. and Panda, KC, Working Capital Management in Public Sector Undertakings of Orissa. *Indian Journal of Public Enterprise,* 4(6) June, 1989. pp. 119-126.

Pandey, RK, State Financial Corporations: Their Audit and Inspections. *Finance and Commerce,* 13(10), 1970, pp. 839-841.

Patel, BI, Working of State Level Public Enterprise: A Case Study of Gujarat Warehousing Corporation. *Institute of Public Enterprise Journal,* (11) 4. pp. 61-66.

Patil, SM, Ominous Time for State Enterprises, *Financial Express,* May 20, 1986, p. 5.

Pillai, NC and Balasubramanian AC, Board of Directors of Public Sector Companies in Kerala — An Analysis. *Lok Udyog,* 17(3) June 1983, pp. 23-34.

Pola, Kumaran, State Government Undertakings: Welfare Ration Shops or Business Enterprises. *Commerce,* 150(3847), 1985, pp. 296-301.

Prabhakara Rao, P, Management Information Systems and Financial Control, Hyderabad, *Institute of Public Enterprises,* 1985, p. 221.

Prasad, Arun, Public Sector Enterprises in Bihar: A Bird's Eye View. *Institute of Public Enterprise Journal* Vol. XI. No. 2, 1988, pp. 41-64.

Prasada Rao P., Management Audit for State Level Public Enterprises: A Case Study of Leather Industry Development Corporation, Hyderabad, *Institute of Public Enterprises,* 1991, 50p.

Pylee, MV, Some Aspects of the Management of India's State

Enterprises. *Indian Journal of Political Science,* January-March, 1963, pp. 1-13.

Raj, HN, Case Studies in Losing State Units. *Business Standard,* June 18, 1980.

Raja, T, Management Problems of Public Sector Undertakings. *Management Perspectives,* April-June, 6(2), 1968, pp. 55-59.

Rajan KA, For Better Performance of Kerala Public Sector. *New Age,* 35(42), October 18, 1987, p. 3.

Ram Prakash, State Enterprises in Rajasthan: Need for Managerial Shake-up. Management in Government, January-March 4(4), 1973, pp. 315-323.

Rajasthan State Enterprises in Action. *Prashasnika,* July-September 1(3), 1972, pp. 37-52.

Rama Krishna, Yerra, Perceptions on the Role of A P Public Enterprises Management Board. Hyderabad, *Institute of Public Enterprise,* 1991.

Rama Rao, UP, APIDC (Andhra Pradesh Industrial Development Corporation) Marches Ahead, *Economic Times,* November 22, 1975, p. 10.

Ramachandran, C, Developpment and Performance of State Level Public Enterprises of Tamil Nadu. *Institute of Public Enterprise Journal,* 11(1), January-March 1986, pp. 24-49.

Ramachandran, MK, Karnataka State Financial Corporation Takes Strides. *Eastern Economist,* November 19, 1976, pp. 1009-1010.

Ramakrishna, KG, Public Enterprises in Mysore State. *Eastern Economist.* October 10, 1969, pp. 687-690.

Ramakrishna Sarma, Infrastructure for Industry: State Role in A.P. State and Society 3(1), 1982, pp. 39-54.

Ramakrishnan, R, Managerial Crisis in State Units. *Economic Times,* December 4, 1972, p. 9.

Ramamurthi, Ravi, Controlling State-owned Enterprises. *Institute of Public Enterprise Journal,* 10(3), 1987, pp. 1-31.

Ranade, CG, Performance of Integrated Milk Cooperatives: A Study of Selected Cooperative Dairies in Gujarat and Maharashtra. Delhi, Concept Publishing, 1988, p. 143.

Ranga Rao, S and Madan Mohan Reddy, V, Governing Boards of State Corporations: A Study of Their Composition in Andhra Pradesh. *Lok Udyog,* December 6(9), 1972, pp. 35-40.

Rao, KV, Management of Working Capital in Public Enterprises, New Delhi, Deep & Deep Publication, 1990, p. 406.

Ratan Reddy, B, Valuation of Hyderabad Allwyn Limited: An Illustrative Exercise. Indian Journal of Public Enterprise, 8(15), December 1993, pp. 21-30.

Ravishankar, S. and Mishra, RK, Improving the Performance of State Level Public Enterprises through Management Training and Development, Lok Udyog 19(3), June 1985, pp. 29-36.

Reddy, BR, Study on Role of Incentives in Generation of Industrial Investment in Andhra Pradesh. Hyderabad, *Institute of Public Enterprise,* 1988. 99p.

Roy, MN, State Financial Corporation: Its Present, Past and Future. Orissa Review, 30(10), 1974, pp. 11-23.

Roy, RC, State Public Enterprise in India. Delhi, Uppal Publications, 1985, p. 393.

Sahay, SN, Financial Management of Public Enterprises. Delhi, S. Chand & Co. Ltd., 1984, p. 216.

Sahu, GN, Management of State Financial Corporation: A Critical Approach. *Indian Journal of Commerce,* 25(3), 1971, pp. 95-103.

Sankar, TL, Mishra, RK and Nandagopal, R, Can State Level Public Enterprises in India Earn a Rate of Return? *Economic and Political Weekly*, 25(47), November 24, 1990.

Do State Level Public Enterprises Need Memorandum of Understanding? *Economic and Political Weekly*, August 31, 1991, pp. M-93-95.

Financial Performance of State Level Public Enterprises in India. Decision, July-September, 1993, pp. 185-203.

Privatisation and Non-privatisation Reforms in State Level Public Enterprises Sectorwise Strategy and Implications. *Indian Journal of Public Enterprise*, 6(11), December, 1991, pp. 131-141.

Role and Relevance of State Level Public Enterprises in 1992. Decision 19(3&4), 1994, pp. 183-214.

State Level Public Enterprises in India: Restructuring for Performance Improvement. *Artha Vijnana*, 35(4), 1993, pp. 301-341.

State Level Public Enterprises in India: An Overview. *Economic and Political Weekly*, August 27, 1994, pp. M-115-119.

Working of State Level Manufacturing Public Enterprises: Promise and Performance. Hyderabad, *Institute of Public Enterprise*, 1991, 8p.

Sankar, TL, Nandagopal, R and Mishra, RK, Management of State Level Public Enterprises in India, Jaipur, Printwell, 1992, 371p.

Performance and Development of State Level Public Enterprises in India. Hyderabad, *Institute of Public Enterprise*, 1989, 215p.

State Level Public Enterprises in India: An Overview. *Economic and Political Weekly*, 24(8), February 25, 1989, pp. 33-40.

Sankar, TL and Pakki Redyy, G, Ranking of Five Indian States. Hyderabad, *Institute of Public Enterprise,* 1992. p. 33+ Annexures.

Sankar, TL, Santana Babu, G and Trivikram, K (Study Team), Andhra Pradesh State Textile Development Corporation: A Study. Hyderabad, Institute of Public Enterprise, 1982.

Saraswathy Rao, Y, Public Enterprises: A State Level Perspective. Delhi, B.R. Publishers, 1986, p. 287.

Sastry, E and Sai, SST, Report on the Study of Schemes Financed by the Andhra Pradesh Backward Classes Cooperative Finance Corporation, Hyderabad, *Institute of Public Enterprise,* 1977.

Satish Chandra T, Legislative Control over Corporate Sector. Jaipur RBSA Publishers, 1994, 215p.

Patterns of Questions on Public Enterprise Trends in Andhra Pradesh Legislative Assembly. Institute of Public Enterprise Journal, 15(1) March, 1992. pp. 55-74.

Satyanarayan Reddy, C and Ramesh Babu, Forms of Financial and Non-financial Assistance, their Sanction and release Process in State Enterprises of Andhra Pradesh. *Journal of Institute of Public Enterprise,* 16(3&4), September & December 1993, pp. 92-105.

Satyanarayana Rao B, Finances of Public Enterprise: A Sample Study of Tamil Nadu State Enterprises. Chartered Accountant, 28(1), 1979, pp. 5-8, 16.

Satyanarayana, S, Role and Vigilance Cell in AP Civil Supplies Department. Hyderabad, *Institute of Public Enterprise,* 1992, p. 64.

Seth, Vijay and Mehta, AR, On the Measurement of State Level Capital Output Ratios. Indian Journal of Industrial Relations, 22(4), April, 1987, pp. 369-390.

Sethuraman, S, Making the Public Sector Profitable. *Industrial Economist,* 20(4), 1987.

Shah, Dilip, Production Functions in Cooperative Dairy Industry of Gujarat. *Indian Journal of Industrial Relations,* 17(3), January 1982, pp. 395-408.

Shah, SG, State Financial Corporations. *Journal of Institute of Bankers* 43(3), 1972, pp. 347-353.

Sharma, GD, Working of State Enterprises in Rajasthan. New Delhi, Sterling Publishers Pvt. Ltd., 1973, 319p.

Sharma, GL, State Industrial Development Corporations: Functions, Working and Problems. *Indian Journal of Commerce,* 25(4), 1972, pp. 455-62.

Sharma, PK, BSIDC (Bihar State Industrial Development Corporation): Promoting Industrial Growth. *Indo-African Trade Journal,* 8(9), 1972, pp. 18-20.

Sharma, P and Singh, SK, Public Enterprises in Bihar: Capital Structure and Financial Returns. *Economic Times,* 6 August, 1973, p. 5.

Shiva Ramu, S, Top Management of State PEs: A Karnataka Study. *Indian Journal of Public Enterprise,* 4(6) June, 1989, pp. 19-30.

Problems of State Public Enterprises: A Karnataka Study. Vikalpa, 9(4), 1984.

Pseudo Management of SLPEs: Perception of Middle Level Executives. Administrative Staff College of India Journal Management, 14(2), March 1985. pp. 187-211.

Shrivastava, NC, Management of State Industrial Undertakings. *Indian Journal of Public Administration,* July-September 7(3), 1961, pp. 345-52.

Shukla, MB, Commercial Viability of PEs in Kerala. *Indian Journal of Public Enterprise,* 4(6), June 1989, pp. 141-150.

State Level Public Enterprises in Bihar: An Outlook for Future. *Indian Journal of Public Enterprise*, 2(3), December, 1987, pp. 70-82.

Shukla, Mata Badal, Structural Framework of Public Sector Industrial Relations (with Special Reference to UP State Government Enterprises). *Lok Udyog*, 18(5), August 1984, pp. 39-43.

Sikidar, Sujit, Accounting and Auditing Practices of Public Sector Units in India. *Indian Journal of Public Administration*, January-March, 1994, pp. 57-62.

Singhvi, GS, Role of Rajasthan Financial Corporation. *Financial Express*, July 31, 1972, p. 13.

Sinha, Raj Kishore, States Undertakings in Bihar and their Profitability. *Bihar Information*, 18(8), 1973, pp. 1-4.

Sinha, UN, Bihar State Agro Industries Development Corporation. *Commerce*, 17 November 1973, pp. 63-67.

Sisodia, VS, Higher Management Seminar on State Enterprises in Rajasthan: A Report. *Prashasnika*, July-September 1(3), 1972, pp. 88-106.

Sivaraman, K, Assistance Rendered by National Cooperative Development Corporation in Karnataka. NCDC Bulletin 9(4), 1975, pp. 20-23.

Srinivasan, NP, Project Formulation in State Enterprises. *Lok Udyog*, 19(6), 1985, pp. 15-20.

State Level Conference of Chairmen and Chief Executives of Enterprises, 11.4.1988.

State Level Conference of Chairmen and Chief Executives of Enterprises, 11.4.1988. n.p. 1988, 300p.

Sukumaran, A, Budgeting in Selected Private and Public Undertakings: A Case Study of Kerala. Delhi, Commonwealth Publishers, 1992, 212p.

Sumathi, Kiyyana Rao, and Prasad, G, Capital Structure in Public Entrprise of Andhra Pradesh. *Institute of Public Enterprise Journal,* 7(2), 1984. pp. 29-41.

Sunil Mani, Technology Profile of A.P. State. A Compendium of Industrial Units in Andhra Pradesh with Foreign Collaboration. Hyderabad, *Institute of Public Enterprise,* 1988.

Suryakumar, K, Labour Relations in Select Andhra Pradesh State Enterprises. *Institute of Public Enterprise Journal.* April-June 1982, pp. 44-53.

Suryanarayana, M, Monograph on Andhra Pradesh State Financial Corporation: A Catalyst of Industrial Development in Andhra Pradesh. Hyderabad, *Institute of Public Enterprise,* 1986, 105p.

Swaminathan, AM, Tamil Nadu Small Industries Corporation Limited, Madras. *Indian Industries,* 17(8-11), 1973, pp. 9-10.

Swamy, K, Finance Performance of Manufacturing State Level Public Enterprises in Andhra Pradesh. (Submitted to Jawaharlal Nehru Technological University). Hyderabad, JNTU, 1993.

Tamil Nadu Industrial Investment Corporation Limited, Tamil Nadu Industrial Investment Corporation Ltd. Setting the Pace for States Industrialisation. *Industrial Economist,* September 15, 1974, pp. 1-5.

Tandon, BC, Public Enterprises in India. Allahabad, Chaitanya Publishing House, 1987, v. 280p.

Tata, Naval H, Role of Western Maharashtra Development Corporation, *Lok Rajya,* August 16, 1972, pp. 46-48.

Thimmaiah, G, Public Sector Units in Mysore: A Critical Appraisal. *Southern Economist,* October 1, 1968 (Special), pp. 9-12.

Tilak, MBG, Overview of Performance of Public Enterprises

of Government of Gujarat. *Institute of Public Enterprise Journal*, 11(2), 1988. pp. 107-123.

Tiwari, RS, Public Undertakings in Madhya Pradesh, Eastern Economist (Annual Number) May 22, 1970, pp. 967-972.

Tiwari, Sharda, Personnel Policies and Industrial Relations in State Level Public Enterprises, Jaipur, Rajasthan, 1988.

Trivedi Prajapathi, Government Enterprises (State Government). *Business Standard*, June 27, 1989.

Vanamala, M, Public Sector Enterprises: An Enquiry into the Corporations for Weaker Sections in Andhra Pradesh. (Submitted to SKK University). Hyderabad, Osmania University, 1989, 263p.

Vanamala, M, Pakki Reddy, G, Uma Shankari and Rasool Saheb, TS (Study Team) Contributions of Public Enterprises to Economic Development of Andhra Pradesh. (Sponsored by Department of Finance, Government of Andhra Pradesh) 2 Vols. Hyderabad, *Institute of Public Enterprise*, 1984.

Valluri, Madhu, Bihar PSUs Continue to Suffer Heavy Loss, State Enterprises. Andhra Shows the Way. *Business Standard*, March 9, 1988, p. 4.

Veerabhadraiah, M, Project Report on Management of Diversification in Public Enterprises: A Case Study of Hyderabad Allwyn Ltd. Hyderabad, *Institute of Public Enterprises*, 1988, p. 134.

Venkaiah, V, Impact of Public Enterprise on Rural Development: A Case Study of Nizam Sugar Factory. *Institute of Public Enterprise Journal*, January-March, 1983, pp. 18-33.

Venkataswamy, G, Ecology of State Government Enterprises: Complexity Causes Ambiguity. *Business Standard*, August 4, 1987, p. 5.

Interface between Government and State Enterprises. Jaipur, Printwell, 1988.

Management of State Government Enterprises in Andhra Pradesh. Hyderabad, Osmania University, 1984.

Management of State Government Enterprises. New Delhi, Archives Publishers, 362p.

Public Policy and Performance of State Public Enterprises: A Comparative Study. *Indian Journal of Public Administration,* October-December 24(4), 1978, pp. 973-989.

State Government Enterprises - I: Factors Curbing Autonomy. *Economic Times,* September 18, 1987.

State Government Enterprises - II: Factors Curbing Autonomy. *Business Standard,* September 19, 1987, p. 5.

State Government Enterprises - II: The Politics of Inefficiency. *Economic Times,* September 1987.

Venkat Rao, CS, State Industrial Development and Investment Corporation. *Commerce,* December, 1974, pp. 181-8.

Venkataratnam, M, Industrial Growth through Andhra Pradesh Industrial Development Corporation. *Financial Express,* December 30, 1974, p. 2.

Venkataswamy, G, Ecology of State Government Enterprises: Complexity Causes Ambiguity. *Business Standard,* August 4, 1987, p. 5.

Interface Between Government and State Enterprises. Jaipur, Printwell, 1988.

Public Policy and Performance of State Public Enterprises: A Comparative Study.

Indian Journal of Public Administration, October-December 24(4), 1978, pp. 973-989.

State Government Enterprises (Bihar): Struggling in the Mire of Loss. *Business Standard,* January 7, 1988, p. 5.

State Government Enterprises (Tamil Nadu): Poor Performance and Mounting Losses. *Business Standard,* December 19, 1987, p. 5.

State Government Enterprise - II : The Politics of Inefficiency. *Economic Times,* September, 1987.

State Government Enterprise - I: Factors Curbing Autonomy. *Economic Times,* September 18, 1987.

State Government Enterprises - II: Factors Curbing Autonomy. *Business Standard,* September 19, 1987, p. 5.

Venkateshwarlu, M, Valuation of State Level Public Enterprises: A Case study of Hyderabad Allwyn. *Institute of Public Enterprises Journal,* 15(2) June, 1992, pp. 111-130.

Vepa, Ram K, State Development Institutions: Need for Coordination. *Lok Udyog,* 2(10), 1969, pp. 1075-1077.

Vijayanna Rao, K., Management of Working Capital with Reference to Selected Andhra Pradesh Public Sector Enterprises, 1969-70 to 1978-1979. Nagarjunanagar, Nagarjuna University, 1982.

Vijayyanna Rao, K and Prasad, G, Andhra Pradesh: Working of State Public Enterprise. *Economic Times,* March 31, 1980.

State Level Public Enterprises in India: How to Stabilise their Finances. *Southern Economist,* 23(16), 1984, pp. 9-12.

Vikramajit, Management Cadre in State Enterprises. *Economic Times,* September 14, 1973, p. 8.

Index

❑❑❑